Autobiography
of an Androgyne

Autobiography of an Androgyne

Earl Lind

MINT EDITIONS

Autobiography of an Androgyne was first published in 1918.

This edition published by Mint Editions 2021.

ISBN 9781513296968 | E-ISBN 9781513298467

Published by Mint Editions®

 MINT
EDITIONS

minteditionbooks.com

Publishing Director: Jennifer Newens
Design & Production: Rachel Lopez Metzger
Project Manager: Micaela Clark
Typesetting: Westchester Publishing Services

Inscribed to NATURE'S STEP-CHILDREN—the sexually abnormal by birth—in the hope that their lives may be rendered more tolerable through the publication of this Autobiography.

"But this is a people robbed and spoiled; they are all of them snared in holes, and they are hid in prison houses; they are for a prey, and none delivereth; for a spoil, and none saith, Restore.

"Who among you will give ear to this? Who will hearken and hear for the time to come?"

—Isaiah XLII, v. 22, 23

Contents

Introduction

I offer no apology for bringing the AUTOBIOGRAPHY OF AN ANDROGYNE before the members of the learned professions, to whom the sale of this book is restricted.

Were, in my opinion, an apology needed, this volume would not make its appearance through my instrumentality.

The reason for its appearance is missionary, and therefore I consider it right and proper that I should explain what I hope to accomplish thereby.

I am sorry not to be able to say that the appearance of this volume will fill a longfelt want.

For, although I hope to fill with the AUTOBIOGRAPHY OF AN ANDROGYNE a void; yet, had this void been recognized, were the want felt to have this void filled, my task would be easier of accomplishment.

The void whereof I speak is the colossal ignorance of the reasons for homosexual practices on one side, and the pharisaical pulchritude on the other side, which, although knowing that homosexuality has been practiced uninterruptedly from biblical times up to the present, refuses to study its causes or its devotees; and while not endeavoring to make this world a better place to live in through its own abandoning unwholesome practices, vices and other actions which, although approved, condoned or ignored by the multitude—because these actions are popular—are condemned by philosophers and thinkers, yet will crucify those whose vices are much less harmful, because they are vices for which this pharisaical pulchritude has no taste, which therefore it cannot understand, and not understanding them, cannot condone.

This is to be no brief in defense of homosexuality, although, were I to try to find redeeming features for homosexual practices in certain cases and under certain circumstances, I would not have to cudgel my brain overly to do so.

This is not intended as a defense of all those who indulge in homosexual practices.

Such a defense might be attempted and successfully carried out, were it possible to bring this question before a jury of unbiased, open-minded and independent thinkers, who would decide the question upon the platform of equal justice to all, weighing the relative harmfulness of all sexual crimes and excesses, and who would not punish those indulging in homosexual practices, if they refuse to punish those indulging in sexual crimes and excesses vastly more injurious to the human race and to society.

This book is published in an endeavor to obtain justice and humane treatment for the Androgynes, that class of homosexualists in whom homosexuality is not an acquired vice but in whom it is congenital.

In pleading a case in Court, even before the highest tribunals, it is good practice not to take it for granted that the judge knows the law, or even facts, which might appear to the pleader to be matters of common knowledge; and so I may be excused if I state to the reader matters which to him may be already familiar.

Let us then first consider what Homosexuality is.

Homosexuality means sexual love for one of the same sex.

Thus, if a male feels sexual desire for another male, or a female for another female, they are called sexually inverted or homosexual.

Freud claims that there is in every one an original bisexual tendency, which is also established anatomically.

Normal development leads from bisexuality to the primacy of the heterosexual instinct.

Thus inversion corresponds to a disturbance of development.

Whether one agrees with Freud, that homosexuality or inversion originates in every instance in early childhood, or whether one disagrees with him and takes the stand which I take, that some cases of homosexuality are congenital, that others are acquired in early childhood, while others again are the result of vice or sexual necessity, as among soldiers, sailors, or in schools; we must come to the conclusion, that laws which do not differentiate in the punishment of crimes against nature between those who are born inverts or whose inversion dates from early childhood and those whose homosexuality is due to vice or association and who amphogenously inverted or occasionally inverted use a sexual object belonging either to the same or the opposite sex, are inadequate, antiquated, not keeping step with the progress which has been made as to the subject, and should be changed.

The subject has been discussed not for tens, or hundreds, but for thousands of years.

Martial, in his epigrams, treats of homosexuality; Socrates and Alcibiades were said to have been lovers; this is the reason why pæderasty is also called Socratic love.

Homosexuality in women is called tribadism, euphemism, Lesbian or Sapphic love; this because Sappho, after having lost Faon, is said to have turned from men to homosexual love.

This should be sufficient to show that homosexuality was discussed among the Romans and Greeks, and it is well known that the Bible is not quiet about it.

Thus then one should expect that a subject which has been so much discussed should be well enough understood to have its devotees treated fairly.

Let us see what the law has to say about it?

While in some countries homosexuality is not punishable, in the United States the law on homosexuality is all comprised in the statutes under the term of Sodomy.

This comprises not only homosexuality, but also bestiality.

The Penal Code of the State of New York, par. 303, says:

Crimes against Nature.

A person who carnally knows in any manner any animal or bird; or carnally knows any male or female person by the anus or by or with the mouth; or voluntarily submits to such carnal knowledge; or attempts sexual intercourse with a dead body is guilty of sodomy and is punishable with imprisonment for not more than twenty years.

Par. 304:

Penetration sufficient.

Any sexual penetration, however slight, is sufficient to complete the crime specified in the last section.

OUR DISCUSSION HAS NOTHING TO do with bestiality or sexual violation of the dead or unnatural practices between persons of different sex.

And here I wish to state that homosexuality between females, or so-called Lesbian or Sapphic love, has, to my knowledge, never been punished in the United States, although the statute seems broad enough to cover certain sexual practices, as for example cunnilingus, between females, while tribadism, in which there is no penetration, and whose devotees according to Yanez, are called in Spain vulgarly "tortilleras," according to the New York Code can not be punished, as there is no penetration. Yanez, in his *Medicina Legal*, published in Madrid in 1884, gives an excellent description of homosexuality and describes also the general appearance of those male homosexualists whose ways and manners resemble those of the female sex, and who in common parlance in the United States are called "Fairies."

Tidy, in his *Legal Medicine*, not only refers, in discussing homosexuality, to Romans, I, 26, but gives some historical references, and cites a number of English cases.

In speaking of "sodomites," he says: "Sodomites are persons of all ages, but they usually present a somewhat feminine appearance, or strive to appear like women. To this end they commonly conceal or destroy, as far as practicable, such virile appendages as beard, whiskers, or moustache, wearing a profusion of jewelry, paint and padding. So far, indeed, may this liking go, that in one case a male to the death is said to have passed himself off as a female, being employed evidently as a passive agent.

"And yet, curious to say, sodomites generally affect the society of their own sex, and avoid that of the opposite sex.

"To them natural sexual intercourse is frequently a matter of absolute distaste... All this suggests the curious question, whether such aberration of sexual desires may not be the result of an incipient hermaphrodism. Casper's account of a brotherhood of sodomites and of their mutual powers of recognition, further suggests to the medical jurist (dangerous as the very idea may be accounted) how far the criminality of these people is not beyond their control. But on the other hand, undoubted sodomites are to be found with none of the characteristics just described and free from all hereditary taint."

I have quoted from Tidy at such length, to show that Tidy recognized the fact that in certain homosexualists a hereditary taint is the cause and because I wish to emphasize the fact that while the condition has been recognized by Tidy and others, yet it has not been clearly understood.

This can be deduced from the words above quoted, that "curious to say, sodomites generally affect the society of their own sex."

It must be understood, that the congenital homosexualist is really a human being, born with the body of a male, with perhaps some female characteristics, but with the soul of a female. The congenital homosexualist always feels himself as a female, and therefore is always attracted towards men and would rather be in their society than in the society of females, who are sexually repulsive to him. This Tidy evidently failed to clearly understand.

This then is my contention, that homosexuality is either an acquired vice, that is to say a habit, or an acquired mental aberration, that is to say, insanity, or congenital; and then it is that a human being is born with a body with sexual organs all those of the male, yet most likely with a body which shows certain earmarks of the female, and with a soul nearly all female, but certainly entirely female in regard to the sex question. Such a person is a homosexualist, because he feels like a woman and to him all male persons belong to the opposite sex. He is not a roué, who has developed homosexuality as a vice, but he is born an androgyne, whom we can recognize in his manners and mannerisms; a male person with female ways.

If then the Bible already speaks of homosexual practices and warns against the idolatrous homosexual practices devoted to Moloch and Bal Phegor; if already Juvenal and Martial and Cornelius Nepos describe homosexuality, were it not about time that something were done to change the existing laws?

Hofman, in his *Lehrbuch der gerichtlichen Medizin*, published in 1884, draws attention to the fact that passive pæderasts are generally of remarkable femininity, and quotes Brouardel as also remarking that this female appearance, these female actions and these female habits, likes and dislikes are generally congenital.

Tidy also, in his work on *Legal Medicine*, published in 1883, states: "Nor must the hereditary nature of such crimes be overlooked."

To quote from Beranger:

> *"Son teint, reluisant de pomade,*
> *Par le carmin est embelli.*
> *On le devine, quand il passe,*
> *Autour de lui l'air est ambré.*
> *Ses cheveux bouclent avec grace,*
> *Son habit presse un dos cambré.*
> *Comme une coquette un peu grasse,*
> *Dans un corset il est serré."*

Mantegazza, in his *Hygiene of Love*, published in 1877, mentions the subject and states that these cases generally are not due to congenital aberration, thus admitting that some of them are. I think that it was in 1877 when Krafft-Ebing first drew attention to the psycho-pathology of certain forms of homosexuality; since that time forty years have passed, and still the laws fail to differentiate between the vicious pæderasts and the unfortunate passive pæderasts. The distinction between those in whom homosexual practices are a vice and in whom they are a misfortune, is, it seems to me, generally very easily made. The vicious homosexualist acts the part of a male. The unfortunate, insane or congenital homosexualist acts the part of a female. The one is active, the other passive.

That the passive homosexualist is a victim of nature, an unfortunate who is generally despised and hounded, seems however not to be enough, for he is also considered legitimate prey of the underworld, who blackmail these unfortunates systematically. This form of blackmail is known under the term of "chantage," and practiced in every large city of the European and American continents. The laws against homosexuality, as at present in force, similar to the Mann White Slave Act, seem to only serve blackmailing crooks, so as to give them an easy living.

It is true that homosexuality at present is not punished as severely as it was in olden times. It was not so long ago when in Europe it was punished by burning, later by burying alive; only a few years ago in the United States it was punishable by hanging; now the punishment is much milder, but, if it be admitted that homosexuality in certain easily recognizable persons is congenital and incurable, and if it be also admitted that it surely is a great deal less harmful than ordinary prostitution, why punish it at all, or why not at least exempt from punishment those homosexualists whom Krafft-Ebing so rightly calls "true stepchildren of nature"?

The author of the Autobiography of an Androgyne called on me some time ago with his manuscript, imploring me to read it and to publish it.

He told me that he had written most of it years ago and that he had spent a great deal of time trying to find a publisher, but unsuccessfully.

He stated that he had written his autobiography in an endeavor to bring his misfortune vividly before the medical and legal fraternities, for the purpose of lightening the heavy load which rested so unjustly, as he said, upon the unfortunates of his class.

While proving to me through letters which were in his possession and which were addressed to him under various pseudonyms, that he had submitted his work to different men of learning, all of whom commented upon it favorably, still the fact that he had unsuccessfully tried to find a publisher among the various publishers of medical works, was not a very good introduction of his manuscript to me; yet the open statement of this fact spoke for his honesty, and although very busy at the time, I promised him that I would read it.

Now a word about the author: While, according to his own statement, he is in the fifth decade, he would pass as considerably younger. I have seen him during the preparation of the work a score of times and have had some slight chance of observing him.

His language was always very carefully chosen and showed considerable polish.

His manner was always very gentlemanly and inoffensive.

In figure he is short, stout and has a very arched back.

His voice is rather hoarse, trembling and has, perhaps, a certain female timbre.

His manner seemed generally timid and embarrassed, and he blushes very easily.

From his appearance and manners he can, by the gnoscenti, be easily recognized as an Androgyne.

His avowed purpose in writing and desiring the publication of his Autobiography, is, as I stated before, by describing his martyrdom, to lighten the burdens which other Androgynes have to bear; yet my study of him makes me think that the underlying and perhaps to him unknown reason for the creation of this Autobiography is vanity.

The author is extremely vain.

My impression of him is, that while he really suffered the agonies he describes; while he really in the beginning of his career underwent the soul struggles he tells about; yet he is at present extremely proud of the, to him undisputable fact, that he is all of a woman's soul in a body which he believes to be one-third female and thus only two-thirds male.

There is no doubt but that his body shows some female characteristics; especially so his breasts.

He glories in it.

To him, this at least is my impression, to be all woman would be heavenly.

Some years ago he underwent the operation of castration.

He says, and perhaps he believes, that the reason why he underwent the operation was, that he suffered from spermatorrhoea.

My belief is, that, feeling as a woman, desiring to be a woman and wishing to seem as much as possible like a woman to his male paramours, he hated above all the testicles, those insignia of manhood, and had them removed to be more alike to that which he wished to be.

I read through his AUTOBIOGRAPHY OF AN ANDROGYNE.

I cannot say that I enjoyed it.

I neither liked the style in which it was written, nor the manner in which, to me, unimportant details were given a great deal of space, nor the manner in which vital questions were entirely overlooked.

I did not see any scientific value in the conversations related nor any poetical value in the verses recited.

The subject matter was all well known to me and nauseating.

I was to edit this "Autobiography" and stood aghast at the task that I thought was before me.

I saw the author and told him what I have just stated and that in my opinion the book had neither literary nor scientific value in the way in which he thought it had.

I found that the author was severely hurt. This Autobiography was his joy—a work which this epoch had been waiting for and which futurity will crown as a classic.

He fought with all his might against any of his verses being omitted. Every single word that I wanted to change or expunge was of vital importance to him.

And then I saw a light.

The AUTOBIOGRAPHY OF AN ANDROGYNE would serve its mission best unedited, and so it practically remains.

The author, in writing this book, has written into it his own soul, for him to read who can see further than the printed word.

He has lighted a torch to show in his own way the baser sex feelings of a sexual invert.

He has shown some of the suffering which he has undergone at the beginning of his career.

He has shown the contempt in which the Androgyne is held by reason of a psychical aberration not of his own making.

He has shown how the homosexualist who does not do because he wills but who does because he must, is exploited by the criminal classes.

In thus lighting the torch and holding it up for us to see what he desires us to see, he also unconsciously lights up himself in all his womanly vanity, showing his pride in the fact that he is different from others; showing his pride in his many conquests; in fact, if I may use the word in a perhaps not quite exact way, giving a *psychoanalysis* of himself without attempting to do so.

Thus then, while the author offers the AUTOBIOGRAPHY OF AN ANDROGYNE as a plain chronological statement of facts slightly covered to hide his identity, I offer it at the same time as a psychological study, well worthy of a careful analysis.

Whether this volume is read from the author's viewpoint or from mine, only one conclusion can be reached:

Such as he are not to be punished.

ALFRED W. HERZOG

October, 1918

Author's Preface

From childhood I have been unusually introspective. I began to keep a diary at the age of fourteen, and have continued it up to past the age of forty almost without intermission. Even my earliest diaries dealt with the phenomena of my sexual life, so that in general I have had to keep them under lock and key.

The third physician from whom I sought a cure for my sexual abnormality gave me to understand as early as 1892 that my case was a remarkable one. This pronouncement incited me still further to keep a record of what life brought me with a view to writing an autobiography some day.

In 1899, at the age of twenty-five, I wrote the accompanying account of my life down to that age, and subsequently added accounts of significant events as they occurred. I also from time to time edited and made inserts in what I had already written. As a result, parts of some pages were written in different years. The book has been fated to wait eighteen years for publication, primarily because American medical publishers—on the basis of the attitude of the profession—have had an antipathy against books dealing with abnormal sexual phenomena.

I wish to impress upon the reader that I have not let the sexual appetite possess first place in my life. It had to have its place, but the appetite itself, exclusive of its effects, occupied only a small place. From this autobiography a hasty reader might obtain the impression that I was completely absorbed in the line of life and thought here presented, that it was all I lived for. But it is to be remembered that the object of the book is to delineate the phenomena of androgynism, passive sexual inversion, and psychical infantilism as they manifested themselves in the life of its writer, and to give only such part of his life as was out of the ordinary. My non-sexual life has been along the same lines as that of all other intellectual workers, and is barely touched upon in this autobiography, that is, only where it has a bearing on the phenomena to be delineated. Taking my adulthood as a whole, the sexual side of life has probably occupied my attention only to the same extent as in the case of the average virile man, although much more than in the case of the average woman.

I am uncertain whether the writing out of my experiences has tended to mitigate my sexual instincts. If it has had any influence in this direction, nearly a score of years has been requisite to make perceptible its curative quality.

My own is not an isolated case. Among most races and in all ages of the world, one individual out of about every three hundred physical males—on a conservative estimate—is by birth predominantly female psychically. I merely furnish an extreme case of passive inversion, and my life experience has simply been unusually varied and noteworthy.

The author trusts that every medical man, every lawyer, and every other friend of science who reads this autobiography will thereby be moved to say a kind word for any of the despised and oppressed step-children of Nature—the sexually abnormal by birth—who may happen to be within his field of activity.

THE AUTHOR

April, 1918

Autobiography of an Androgyne

Hermaphroditos

The fusion in one human being of the distinctive physical and mental characteristics of the two sexes has from antiquity proved to be a phenomenon interesting to mankind. In some of the great museums of the world can still be seen examples of the classical statue of *Hermaphroditos*, with complete primary male sexual determinants and no trace of female, but with female secondary determinants. The work now in the hands of the reader portrays the inner history and the life experience of such a specimen of the *genus homo.*

An "hermaphrodite," according to the original Greek signification of this term, was not an individual—in the modern sense—having both the male and the female organs of reproduction in whole or in part, or a curious fusion of the two, but only those of the male. In other respects, however, the bodily form was that of a female. The hermaphrodite was thus, according to the Greeks, a female with male genitals. Because modern usage has diverted the term "hermaphrodite" to a different signification, the word "androgyne" has come into use to denote an individual with male genitals, but whose physical structure otherwise, whose psychical constitution, and *vita sexualis* approach the female type.

Androgynes have of course existed in all ages of history and among all races. In Greek and Latin authors there are many references to them, but these references are not always understood except by the few scholars who are themselves androgynes or at least passive sexual inverts. About the middle of the 16th century, the celebrated theologian Beza more clearly wrote: "What shall I say of these vile and stinking *androgynes*, that is to say, these men-women, with their curled locks, their crisped and frizzled hair?"[1] As is evident in this passage, these men-women, because misunderstood, have been held in great abomination both in the middle ages and in modern times, but the prejudice against them was not so extreme in antiquity, and a cultured citizen having this nature did not then lose caste on this account.

But until Krafft-Ebing published his epoch-making work, *Psychopathia Sexualis*, in the last decade of the 19th century, European

---

1. Harmar's translation of Beza, page 173.

and American medical science was either practically ignorant of or else ignored the existence of androgynism. But that author treated principally of other unusual sexual phenomena. Very little of androgynism came under his observation. I quote from page 389 of the English translation of the 12th edition of his work: "There is yet wanting a sufficient record of cases belonging to this interesting group of women in masculine attire with masculine genitals."

The present work discloses not only the life of an androgyne *per se*, but that of a "fairie" or "petit-jesus," the life of which rare human "sport" (in the biological sense) your author was apparently also predestined to live out in a way immeasurably more varied than falls to the lot of the ordinary fairie, having had a limited experience in this vocation in Berlin and Paris and other great European cities, in addition to his extensive experience in New York.

The "fairie" is a youthful androgyne or other passive invert (for they are perhaps not all members of the extreme class of androgynes) whom natural predestination or other circumstances led to adopt the profession of the fille de joie. The term "fairie" is widely used in the United States by those who are in touch with the underworld. It probably originated on sailing vessels of olden times when voyages often lasted for months. While the crew was either actually or prospectively suffering acutely from the absence of the female of the species, one of their number would unexpectedly betray an inclination to supply her place. Looked upon as a fairy gift or godsend, such individual would be referred to as "the fairy." As the author is one of the first users of the printed word in this derived sense, he has elected to adopt a distinctive spelling.

It is hardly necessary to explain that the sacrilegious term, "petit-jesus," commonly used in France, means "a little Jesus." This term would naturally be applied to youthful pathics by the irreverent because being psychically female, they are likely to be "saintly" or "goody-goodies," as were both your author as a youth, and practically all the youthful pathics he has known.

Contrary to the ordinary view, there exists, in the human race, no sharp dividing line between the sexes, just as there exists none between the vegetable and the animal kingdoms. The two sexes gradually merge into each other. Between the complete physical and psychical man and the similarly complete woman, there are innumerable stages of transitional individuals. As there are organisms which the novice would be puzzled to classify as animal or vegetable, so there are human beings who have a just claim to be classed with the sex other than that with which they are commonly classed. Some examples of these transitional individuals are the psychical hermaphrodite, the pseudo-hermaphrodite, the mujerado of the Mexican Indians, the man-woman of East India, and the virago or amazon, as well as the fairie, already mentioned.

Besides the fact of the existence of the decidedly hermaphroditic or androgynous types named, there exists a continuous scale of mental sexuality along which all human beings might be arranged, the poles of which are thorough masculinity and thorough femininity, respectively. At the masculine pole stand the warrior, the blue-jacket, the pugilist, etc., and it was only such, the tremendously virile, who possess no gentle or feminine traits at all, to whom your author was ordinarily attracted. Further down the male side of the scale, after the man of adventure and sport, come, successively, the stevedore and his like, the manual laborer, and the merchant, and still lower, the scholar, which class possesses in general only a comparatively low degree of masculinity and virility. Partaking largely of the feminine type of mind are the male dress-maker and milliner, and the dilettante.

Those at the extremity of the male side of the scale, as the volunteer soldier and sailor, are the most strongly inclined to venery, as a general rule. This is your author's conclusion after intimate experience with 800 young men, of whom at least one-half belonged to the occupations just designated. He concludes further from his experience that nearly all who associate with a fairie belong to this "tremendously virile" class. It is also probably true that congenital active pederasts belong chiefly to this class. The individuals near the lower end of the male side of the scale, as the college professor, are as a rule continent by birth, and fathers of few children, while those at the lower end, as the male milliner and the dilettante, are likely to be sexual inverts. Your author happens to be a pronounced specimen of the dilettante.

At the beginning of the feminine side of the scale, and likely also to be inverts, stand the woman soldier (surreptitious), the woman marksman, and the woman gymnast. Lower down stands the ordinary *mater familias*, entirely normal sexually and completely satisfied with monandry. The *fille de joie* stands still lower, and is as a rule more intensely feminine and childlike than the *mater familias*. Many are also naturally polyandrous. At the feminine pole we find the helpless cry-baby species of woman. The author aspired to be of this type, and always, when impersonating a woman, acted out this type.

As already indicated, the participation of the transitional individuals in the characters of the two sexes varies in all degrees. There may be simply a union of the perfect body of one sex with the susceptibility to such sexual charms as ordinarily attract the other sex alone, or with the mental traits of the other sex. Or the individual may possess the male genitals, but be beardless, or else possess mammary glands, broad pelvis, and sacral dimples; or possessing the female genitals, have a rudimentary moustache, or else meagrely developed breasts, narrow pelvis, etc. Instances have been known of human beings with an ovary on one side of the body and a testicle on the other, and of males who were able to suckle infants.

As to my own feminine characteristics, I have been told by intimate associates from boyhood down to my middle forties—when this book goes to press—that I markedly resemble a female physically, besides having instinctive gestures, poses, and habits that are characteristically feminine. My schoolmates said that I would make a good-looking girl and that kissing me was "as good as kissing a girl." When I was fourteen, one of them remarked that my calves were "as shapely as those of a girl." My associates in college have remarked how much I was like a woman in form and manners, though they never showed evidence of a suspicion that I might be an invert. They were probably ignorant of the existence of this human sport. "He blushes like a woman," was said of me. Later, in my fairie days, my associates would remark that my hands felt like a woman's, and that my skin in general was as soft as a woman's. They said that my voice, especially when singing, had a feminine timbre. The voice is one of the chief criteria by which to determine abnormal sexuality. I fancy that I can diagnose a man sexually simply by hearing him sing. For example, a male invert, as well as the closely related "eunuch by birth" or anaphrodite, is likely to sing a tenor which is hardly distinguishable from an alto.

I have been told that my speaking voice is a very uncommon one, having the "fulness of a woman's voice," and that it often "breaks and changes, sometimes in the middle of a sentence; from being masculine, it suddenly changes timbre and becomes decidedly feminine." I have myself observed sometimes when in conversation with a young man with whom I was in love that my voice would involuntarily change from a bass to a treble. My voice has also been described as "soothing, sentimental-sounding, gushing, bland, and caressing." I have been told that when I talk, involuntary—and to myself unconscious—movements of the lips take place not necessary for articulation, and that the same movements take place occasionally even when I am not talking.

Barbers have remarked that my hair is "literally as fine as silk," that they had "never seen it so fine in any other man." I believe this to be a general peculiarity of androgynes, who also have a predilection for wearing the hair rather long because they think it contributes to their own good looks, while abhorring long hair in a normal male.

I have the feminine slope of shoulders and the feminine angle of arm. Pelvis is broad and limbs loosely hung, as in a woman, and fingers and hands rather feminine in their general fineness of texture, comparative absence of hair, absence of prominent bones and veins, and the softness and pleasing tint of skin.

Features are small like a woman's, but nose, lips, and ears large in proportion, indicating sensuality. I possess mammary glands and sacral dimples. While my breasts are as large as in some women, the nipples are small, even for a man. I am small-boned, of delicate build, and my muscular system is soft. An anatomist of national reputation who gave me a physical examination at the age of thirty-three, pronounced approximately one-third the exterior lines of my body those of the female, and remarked that any one viewing my naked form from the rear and not knowing my sex, would pronounce me a female.

I was said not to "reason like a man, that is, logically"; to be "fussy and inclined to peevishness"; and to have "great patience for minute details."

I was said to throw a ball, drive a nail, etc., "just like a girl." A lead pencil sharpened by me looks as if I had chewed it off with my teeth. I have always had the feminine instinct of screaming at slight provocation. When coasting as a child, I always sat upright after the manner of girls. In snowball fights, in which the girls packed the snowballs behind the barrier and the boys exposed themselves in throwing, I instinctively took my place with the girls, the eternal lack of fitness never dawning upon me.

I might mention here some further characteristics which are not peculiarly feminine. I am below the average stature for a man, and unusually light for my volume, weighing only 110 pounds stripped from the age of nineteen to twenty-five, after I had attained my maximum height of five feet five inches. My back is much arched. Penis is below the average size, but entirely normal. Testicles were pronounced of normal appearance by the surgeon who castrated me at the age of twenty-eight.

I am of the brunette type. At the age of eighteen, the growth of hair on my body and limbs became more luxuriant than on the average male, but after the first shaving off of all this hair in my early fairie-days, I continued to be far less hairy than the average man even after I ceased the practice of body-shaving.

My lips are a deep red, and my complexion gives the appearance of good health. My eyes are bistre-brown. I have been told that I look like a woman around the eyes, and when youthful have been complimented on their beauty, and my general appearance pronounced not unprepossessing. I have been pursued by women, and have received three proposals of marriage. In general the women who have seemed to be attracted toward me have been a few years older than myself. Havelock Ellis has said ("Sexual Inversion," page 140) that "women seem with special frequency to fall in love with disguised persons of their own sex." Your author is really a woman whom Nature disguised as a man.

As late as my middle forties my "childlike face" has been commented upon, and even more my "decidedly childlike manner." I have been told that my "face wears expressions not ordinarily seen on persons of (my) age," that in the office my childishness is a constant source of mirth with my business associates, even those who have not had the faintest idea that I am sexually abnormal and even addicted to fellatio, and that they watch me while I am working because of my childlike way of doing things and my childlike expression. According to one of my business-associate informants, I still had in my middle thirties "the real childlike naiveté." The term "grownup child" has also been affectionately applied to me by my office associates down to my middle forties, and they have said that teasing me was "just like teasing a child." All through my life, even down to my middle forties, when this book goes to press, my male school or business associates—most of whom have not even suspected my inversion—have taken delight in teasing me as older children a younger child, or as brothers tease their sisters, and I generally liked to be thus teased.

My office associates in a "provincial" city in my middle thirties were far more puritanical and unsophisticated than those in New York City of my middle forties, and never gave any evidence that they even knew of the existence of fairies. But those of the later period showed such knowledge, and several times made remarks to me indicating their suspicions about myself, but I always sought to counteract them. The knowledge of unusual sexual phenomena is apparently far more widespread in a great cosmopolitan center like New York than in a "provincial" city.

Further, all my life down to my early thirties, my decidedly virile associates in school and business have babied me. Indeed in some respects I have never ceased to be a baby mentally. I have wept and sobbed a great deal all my life. Up to my early thirties, I yearned to be called "Baby" by decidedly virile males, and to have them treat me as a baby and a weakling. All through my open career as a fairie, I conducted myself with intimates in the same way as a baby of two years towards its mother. Whenever I have seen an infant nursing, I have been seized with a desire for fellatio cum viro of about my own age, and have sometimes even experienced an attack of babyish actions, as panting or cooing in satisfaction, or swayed the head or other parts of the body, a sort of natural graceful dance of these parts. I seem to have retained many of the instincts of the babe which are normally outgrown; only these instincts—the feeling of dependence, the looking for protection, the yearning to be held in the arms and fellatio (in its etymological sense)—were, after the age of four, no longer directed to the mother, but to stalwart males around my own age.

I have aged slowly, successfully passing for twenty-four as a fairie after I had reached thirty-one, and for twenty-nine in my middle forties. When I was thirty-two, a lady of forty who did not know my age remarked of me: "Why he is only a boy!" When I was forty-two, a business associate of rather long-standing and only twenty-six years of age remarked that he had "never met any one else so abnormal as (myself) in respect to the discrepancy between apparent and actual age." I have sometimes thought of myself as "the boy who never grew to be a man." Before reaching my fortieth year, it was my ambition to preserve my youth indefinitely. In my middle forties business associates have asked me for the recipe for perennial youth. Before reaching my fortieth year, possibly no other male was so horrified as myself at the thought of waning youth and approaching old age. But now (1918), in my middle forties, I am reconciled to growing old.

Why am I a sexual invert? I have an explanation to offer, which is perhaps more fanciful than scientific. Is there not a difference between the "protoplasm" or cellular tissue of males and of females, which is the ground of the difference in the physical and psychical development of the sexes? Must there not be in the protoplasm of males a specific male "germ" or characteristic, and in the protoplasm of females a different germ, which are the ground of the opposite development of the sexes? Just as we know by the taste that the protoplasm of the muscle of an ox is differently constituted from that of a sheep, likewise must not that of the male and female homo differ, although in less degree? If through a surgical operation the breast from a male infant could be grafted in the proper place on a female infant, and the breast from a female infant on a male infant, the two individuals, as they became adult, would develop physically along the lines of his or her own sex except the grafted breast. That of the girl would remain flat, that of the boy would develop a mammary gland and become elevated into a mons. They each have on them a patch of the tissue of the opposite sex. In the passive invert there may exist one or more such patches from birth.

According to the author's theory,—whether any individual shall be a male or a female depends on the result of a battle in the embryo between the female corpuscles or germs of the egg and the male of the spermatozoa. From some cause, perhaps the relative state of vitality of the secretory sexual glands at the time of the formation of the particular egg and spermatozoon, either the female germs or the male germs happen to be the more vigorous, and determine the sex of the unborn. If the fœtus develops into a female, it is because the female germs have devoured the male. For some reason, in exceptional cases, the more vigorous set of cells have not succeeded in devouring the other set entirely, and both kinds coexist in different parts of the same individual throughout his existence. In a male there may be only a single patch of female tissue—that is, tissue dominated in its development by the presence of the female bacteria—about the cheeks and neck, rendering him beardless, but with masculine habits of mind and the male sexual instinct. To constitute a passive invert, the brain, the physical basis of the psychical nature, must be composed of female tissue, must be a "female brain."

Can it be denied that the brain of a male is fundamentally different from that of a female, although in outward appearance they are practically alike? The psychical nature of a female is radically different from that of a male, consequently the fundamental nature of certain brain cells of the female must be as different from that of corresponding cells of the male as the psychical nature of a woman is different from that of a man, and as the corpus of a woman is different from that of a man. How can one explain why a six-year-old boy (the author) should class himself as a girl, give himself a girl's name, fight against his parents' course of bringing him up as a boy, and grieve because he could not be brought up as a girl, except on the assumption that the cells of his brain were identical with the cells of a girl's brain and fundamentally different from those of a normal boy?

If a surgeon could interchange the brains of a boy and of a girl, your author believes that the boy would ever afterward feel himself to be a girl, and the girl feel herself to be a boy. But it would be nearer the truth to say that with the implanting of the brain of the opposite sex, the male and female souls were also transposed. We would have an instance of a male human being with a perfect female body except the brain—an artificial amazon. Similarly, a female human being with a perfect male body except the brain—an artificial androgyne. In the natural androgyne, the female brain was formed in the male corpus before birth. There are likely, as in the case of your author, to be other patches of female tissue in other parts of the corpus.

"Active inverts," improperly so called, have been referred to as cases of "a female mind in a male body," as in the Introduction to Eekhoud's "Escal Vigor." The subject of this novel, as well as Oscar Wilde, whose case evidently forms the theme of the book, were not such instances. Theirs were cases of innate and therefore irresponsible sexual perversion rather than of inversion. They were "urnings." "Escal Vigor" is of value as portraying the development and inner life of the urning, while this autobiography deals with the passive invert, or "the invert" properly speaking. The urning or active pederast loves an adolescent as a normal man loves a woman, and desires active paedicatio or else mutual onanism. The passive invert loves the adolescent as a woman loves a man, and desires fellatio, or occasionally the part of the pathic in paedicatio.

While reading "Escal Vigor" many years ago, your author was convinced that the book was primarily written by Oscar Wilde and based on his own life experience. This suspicion is confirmed by the name of the book, the two words having the same length as those of the name of the individual; the second and third letters of the first name being the same in both, as well as the second letter of the surname;

while the initial V is the French equivalent of the English W, the novel having been first published in French. I have myself built a pseudonym on my baptismal name in similar fashion. The suspicion is further confirmed by the rumor of 1918 that Wilde is still alive.

There occur homosexual practices which are really due to moral depravity or to the absence of the opposite sex. This is the true sodomy, an entirely different phenomenon than is present in the case of the congenital invert and urning. Knowledge of the history of the particular individual will readily determine to which of the three categories he belongs.

The author's criticism of Havelock Ellis's theory "that a condition of diffused minor abnormality in physical structure, consisting in approach to the feminine type, is the basis of congenital inversion; that inversion is bound up with a modification of the secondary sexual characters" is that in my own case the attraction toward the male sex was powerful as early as the age of three, when there is probably no difference between the physical type of the normal and of the inverted male. This indicates that there is no cause-and-effect relation between the feminine secondary sexual characters and the love for the male sex, but that they are twin effects of a common cause, namely, the presence in the male body of the particular kind of governing corpuscles or germs ordinarily found only in the protoplasm of females.

The girl-boy with diffused minor abnormality in physical structure, consisting in approach to the feminine type, is rather a female who has, along with some other male structures, developed testicles and penis in place of the usual ovaries and cunnus. Here it is not so much a case of a female brain in a male body, but of the female brain in a *female* body with various abnormal developments along the line of male structure. A girl-boy is sometimes even physically perhaps more a female than a male, although the primary sexual determinants and some of the secondary sexual characters are those of the male sex.

In a manner similar to that described by Kurella, the author believes the invert is a transitional form between the complete male or the complete female and the sexually undifferentiated homo seen in the early fœtus.

Practically it is all right, but medico-legally it is wrong, to make the genitals the universal criterion in the determination of sex. Medico-legally, sex should be determined by the psychical constitution rather than by the physical form. There are thousands of physical females

Men call the invert's instincts vice. The invert has just as much reason for calling the normal man's instincts vice when they are not exercised solely in order to create a new human being. It is only a case of the pot calling the kettle black. In the eyes of the Supreme Being, with whom innate and unreasoning disgust is not a factor, the instincts of the normal man and of the invert are on a par morally and æsthetically. There is no ground for the charge that the passive invert's practices are aimed at the very existence of the race. In the first place, Nature made him psychically impotent from birth. In the second place, his practices could not be spread by example. They are regarded by all normally constituted males with such disgust and aversion that practically no one would stoop to them except those born with the peculiar cravings. And why place a heavy penalty on one particular practice which might prevent a few births, and give large liberty to other practices with a hundred and a thousand fold more power to diminish the birth rate? The author was addicted to sensuality more than the vast majority of inverts. Nevertheless, if he had never yielded to instinct, there would not be today a single human being more in the world than there are. None of his intimates were given to begetting children, at least on the threshold of manhood, which was the age at which they consorted with him.

The invert's harmless instinctive sexual conduct (generally fellatio, seldom paedicatio) is today regarded as a felony almost throughout Christendom. France, Italy, and Holland are the only Christian nations which have entirely repealed the laws enacted against these unfortunates during the Dark Ages. Old English law provided that the guilty one be burnt alive, while other statutes of the same law condemned him to be buried alive. In the reign of Richard III, he was hanged. The death penalty was not abolished until after the reign of George IV. At the present time in England, the maximum penalty is penal servitude for life, and the minimum, ten years imprisonment. In the United States the penalty is from five to twenty years imprisonment. Is it not unjust to keep on the statute books these laws against an unfortunate and harmless class?

I am here reminded of two conferences with Mr. Anthony Comstock, because part of his business while alive was that of hunting down inverts and haling them off to prison. By the irony of fate, I was during my college days nicknamed after this gentleman because on hearing an obscene remark by a fellow student, my features involuntarily expressed shock and disapproval, probably due to my having the mind of a woman.

In this autobiography, I may sometimes refer to myself as "Ralph Werther." At the beginning of my career as "Jennie June," when asked for my real name, I answered "Raphael Werther," since I did not wish to bring disgrace on my family name. I adopted the name "Raphael" because of its euphony and glorious associations; the name "Werther," because like Goethe's hero I was doomed to great sorrow through the passion of love. During my first two years in college, when I often meditated suicide, and was by far the unhappiest person in the college community, Goethe's "Sorrows of Werther," the romance of suicide, had a peculiar fascination for me. Later I substituted "Ralph" for "Raphael" since I found the latter sounded too "stagey" to be believed.

The author may be accused of copying the pen-name of Mrs. Croly in the name that he gave himself when undertaking the role of a girl. But I was not conscious of the existence of this pen-name until after I had selected "Jennie June." In early childhood I had called myself "Jennie," always my favorite girl's name. It has always seemed to me the most feminine of names. I adopted the name "June" because of the alliteration, the beauty of the word, and its agreeable associations. It was first suggested to me while reading one of Cooper's novels, where it appears as the name of a gentle, extremely feminine squaw. It was suggested to me secondly by my seeing it appear as a surname on the sign of a business house.

At the beginning of my career as a fairie, I debated for some time whether the name of my feminine personality should be "Jennie June," "Baby," "Pussie," or the name of a particular one of the foremost prima donnas of history. I enjoyed hugely being called "Baby" by young men. A strange young ruffian one day passed me on the street, and addressed me jocularly: "Hello Pussie!" I cannot express how much it pleased me, and I longed to be called "Pussie" always. As to my impulse to copy the name of the prima donna, I would have day dreams of being such a personage. At the opera I would imagine myself as identified with the leading soprano—that I was she. As is usual with professional fairies, I sought to cultivate a soprano singing voice, though singing a baritone when in my every-day circle.

The fourth child of my mother's eleven children, I was born and passed my first sixteen years of life in the most refined section of a large village within fifty miles of New York City. At the time of my birth, each parent was about thirty years of age. My mother appears to have married for money rather than for love. My parents, and indeed all adults who had a molding influence over my early life, were eminently respectable religious people.

I know the history of my stock for several generations back. No member of any of the several families whose blood is mingled in my veins was ever arrested. With the exception of several black sheep, the several families have been composed of exceptionally pious people.

Both my paternal and maternal stock have been very prolific. No relative has ever distinguished himself by reason of his intellect or otherwise, the men having been exclusively farmers or retail merchants. I am perhaps the most intellectual individual that has appeared in the several families. My father was the shrewdest man and the most successful at making money of any member of these several families.

The following are the only bad strains which I have been able to find in my blood: A maternal great-great-great uncle was half-witted. A maternal great-great uncle was a worthless character, but a good singer, going around from tavern to tavern singing for his grog. Perhaps that is the development a fairie took in his environment. A maternal great uncle, though a good business man, became intoxicated occasionally. A paternal great uncle was half-witted. A maternal second cousin was mildly insane for at least several years. A paternal and also a maternal uncle, besides being extreme dipsomaniacs, lacked the energy to earn their own living, and also never married. The fact that the paternal uncle used to fondle me excessively while I was a boy ten to twelve years of age and hold me clasped in his embrace in such a way as would at the present writing suggest to me that he entertained thoughts of paedicatio, indicates that he was possibly an active pederast. The maternal uncle was known, while in his early twenties, to have indulged in solitary onanism before boys around the age of twelve, but all his adult life he appeared to be unusually attracted toward girls aged from ten to twelve, but I do not believe he ever corrupted any, as he was always popular in his community.

A female first cousin is a psychical hermaphrodite, and while married to a man, has always retained a woman sweetheart, who has evidently occupied a place in my cousin's affections much above the husband. From my close observation of this case for over thirty years,

I am convinced that normal women succumb more readily to the advances of a gynander than do normal men to those of an androgyne. The cousin is decidedly masculine both physically and psychically. No offspring resulted from her marriage.

The question has been much discussed as to whether sexual inversion is congenital or acquired. In my own case—as well as in that of my female cousin—it is indubitably congenital. The full evidence, in addition to my decidedly feminine anatomy and her decidedly masculine, may not be presented here out of regard for others.

My very earliest memories are those of following out my strong baby's instinct for the nipple—immediately after I was weaned—by making use of the best substitute that came in my way. Pueri, atque puellae, several years older than myself, with whom I was intimately thrown every day, furnished me with what nature craved. The infant's nursing instinct unfortunately did not die out in me as in the normal individual, but has continued powerful all my life, though with transferred object. Once after I had grown up—much to my shame—my mother remarked before a small family gathering that until I was quite a large boy (perhaps nine years of age) I would in my sleep go through imbibing motions, like an infant at the nipple.

My earliest memory of all of this perversion of the nursing instinct and its transformation into a perverted sexual instinct is the following: A large carpet hung over a line. Several girls around eleven years of age sat down inside and exposuerunt pudenda. The conversation was about the boys, who they wished might come in. I was hardly more than a baby and was undoubtedly thought too young to understand or disclose their conduct. I crept from one to another, os cunnis earum. I was too young to know that it was the organ of micturition, or to distinguish between it and the breast. My instinct was sugere when the latter was presented to me, and I did the same to it. Possibly the girls told me to.

Only on one other occasion, at the age of six, did I have such relations with a female. The girl, of my own age, begged it of me, much to my disgust. But I had innumerable relations cum pueris. The earliest remembered occurred when I was three-and-a-half years old. A boy of nine had myself, a brother of five, and another of fifteen months sugere penem erectum. For several years he sought me occasionally for the same purpose. My two brothers complied only a few times, while I eagerly grasped every opportunity. They developed into strong, virile, six-foot men, husbands and fathers.

One other boy, a year older than myself, became an even greater favorite. From my fifth to seventh year, our relations were almost as intimate as those of a husband and wife. We used to play "husband and wife," although the fact of conjugal relations was the farthest from our thoughts. When I reached the age of seven, our relations ceased, since we were sent to different schools and he began to play with normal boys, while I henceforth shared the pastimes of the little girls and had them almost exclusively for my companions. In subsequent years of our boyhood, he asked for fellatio several times, but I refused through shame.

My addiction was common knowledge among the boys, and others sought it. While engaged in games with boys, sometimes fellatio would occur every few minutes. Before reaching the age of seven, I had doubtless had more than one thousand such experiences. I of course always took the more humiliating part. Only once in my life, at the age of thirty-six, has another taken that part with me, much to my disgust. Out of nearly 800 intimates during my lifetime, only one ever sought to take that part.

I told these boy playmates to call me "Jennie," and encouraged them to use sexual argot to me. I instinctively hid all my sexual experiences from everybody except my boy intimates, though some of them proclaimed my addiction abroad in my hearing and much to my shame. Only once my mother questioned me suspiciously as to why I entered an outhouse every little while with my boy friend, but I counteracted her suspicion.

I was decidedly the greatest cry-baby of my mother's eight children who survived infancy, as well as the most weakly. I was the only child of the neighborhood subject to convulsions, but these were not more than half a dozen in number and occurred before the age of six. As early as the age of three I suffered from occasional melancholia, and would bang my head on the floor and express the wish that "I was dead." A girl-boy acquaintance committed suicide at the age of twelve by swallowing rat poison.

I was the only girl-boy of my immediate neighborhood, and from the seventh to the twelfth year of my life, was looked upon by all the other children as more girl than boy. When, after the age of seven, I made acquaintances farther off than in my own block, I became acquainted with three other girl-boys on three adjacent blocks, and a number of others in the village. It was common knowledge among the boys of the school. After they became adults, three became notorious among the sporting adolescents of the village, as I learned through a brother who belonged to that class.

The only one with whom I was intimate became, between the ages of fifteen and twenty, a regular fille de joie. A coterie of particularly virile adolescents who had no other means of satisfying their libido, and who were disinclined to visit an evil resort, had recourse to him regularly that he might take the humiliating role in fellatio. Young inverts who do not repress their instincts have relations ordinarily with their young male friends. I was an exception in this respect, as well as in respect to conscientious scruples against following instinct.

My other two girl-boy playmates became, respectively, an organist and an orchestra leader by profession when they became adult. During their late teens and early twenties, they had many liaisons (fellatio) with sport-loving young men—according to my brother—but having more money than the invert just described, they played the wooer, being the seeker, and choosing their intimates, instead of being sought out by the many. They spent a considerable part of their earnings on their beaux. I know nothing about the sexual conduct of any of these three inverts after they passed the age of twenty-five. But the first mentioned developed into a notorious dipsomaniac toward middle age, and the other two, when past the age of forty, are healthy, prosperous, and I believe well esteemed in their community. Most of their business associates have never heard anything against them. Of course none of the three ever married a *woman.*

Of this group of passive inverts who grew up together, I alone had the scholarly instinct and was unusually religious. Of the six who lived to be adults, three—including the organist and the orchestra leader—had extraordinary talent as musicians. No growth of beard ever showed itself on the face of one of the three, and he looked remarkably like a woman.

My knowledge of these inverts leads me to remark at this point that in general those who have relations with a passive invert are normal young men who later marry a woman, but in whom the fire of lust has been kindled by nature subsequent to puberty and for whom circumstances prevent marriage between eighteen and twenty-five years of age.

Every large city block and almost every small village of the world has its girl-boy, so far as my wide observation goes. After a life extending over nearly half a century and spent in many countries of the world, it is my own careful estimate that approximately *one physical male in three hundred* is born with this nature.

Physicians possibly have not discovered inverts in such numbers: First, because the majority of the medical profession have been in almost entire ignorance of the existence of this variety of the *genus homo,* and have therefore neglected to search around for them; and secondly, because of the fact that through humanity's misunderstanding and persecution of them, these inverts hide their idiosyncrasies and secret practices as no other class of mankind. They can be discovered only by careful search, and recognized only by those having an intimate knowledge of the invert's character and habits. They are often unsuspected even by their own families.

In a class of fifty boys in a school, there was one passive invert. In another class of forty, there were two. In a club of thirty young men, there were two. In an office-staff of fourteen, there were two. In a community of twelve hundred inhabitants, six were known to your author. Havelock Ellis has stated that among the professional and most cultured classes of England, the number of "homosexualists"—which term includes active pederasts as well as passive inverts—may rise as high as one in twenty. Moll has stated that he knew of from 850 to 1,050 in Berlin alone, which would make the ratio one to every 1,666 inhabitants. Of course Moll could know of only a small proportion of the total number in Berlin.

All inverts do not give way to their instincts, since the strength of these instincts varies in different individuals, as does the degree of effeminacy, just as there are corresponding differences in normal individuals. Your author's is an extreme case of passive inversion. His case is also unusual because of the strange combination of appetencies in one individual: the instincts of the fairie, the thirst for knowledge of the savant, the yearning after God and holiness of life of the zealot, and the impulse toward altruism of the missionary. My intention from the age of fifteen to nineteen to pass my life as a foreign missionary and preacher of the Gospel was relinquished because inconsistent with the much stronger appetency of the fairie, which finally carried all good resolutions before it.

I grew up slowly, and when adult was the shortest of my parents' eight children. Six-foot men are common among my near relatives, especially my brothers, but I am five feet five inches. At six years of age I was smaller than a brother of four. In college I was noticeably small and of slight build, weighing only 110 pounds stripped when I graduated.

My first impression of the stern realities of life came at the age of six when my parents insisted on putting me in breeches. I wanted to wear skirts all my life. I shrunk from going out in distinctively male garb, and dodged behind the trees when I discovered an acquaintance approaching. The sensation was almost as painful as if I had been compelled to walk the streets naked. Until I reached my early thirties, I did not cease to regret being compelled to taboo feminine apparel, and was constantly being criticised by members of my family for choosing bright colors and as fancy apparel as a male can possibly wear. Androgynes have a predilection for such apparel, just as gynanders prefer the severely plain. Dress is one of the best signs by which to judge whether any suspected individual is or is not an invert. From the age of seven to twelve I occasionally masqueraded in a sister's dress, coquetting with my boy acquaintances the same as if I were physically a girl.

After reaching the age of seven, I abstained from fellatio on account of shame, as well as because I now habitually played with girls. Nevertheless, as just indicated, I was more crazy after the boys than any of my companions, and was a great flirt. When, promenading with a party of girls, we would encounter boys of our acquaintance, I would incite them to chase myself and the girls. With the girls I would discuss the merits of the various boys and name my favorites. The girls did not look upon me as a boy. Only one ever asked me to take the normal boy's part in coitus, and I answered naïvely and without embarrassment that I did not know how. My family would ridicule me for playing with the girls, but that did not stop it.

Up to the age of twelve I continued to tell my most intimate schoolmates to call me "Jennie," encouraged them to hug me, and right in the school-room reclined in their bosoms because of amorousness. Several would hug and kiss me right in school, and in private request fellatio, but I always turned from the latter proposition in shame. To yield would have been my highest earthly pleasure, but I could not bear the disgrace. Mean-spirited boys would call me a girl in derision, and twit me about my conduct of early childhood, thus awakening a violent desire to commit suicide.

I was as fond of dolls as is a little girl. Two other characteristic pastimes were playing preacher and playing school, generally all by myself. I spent a large part of my time in the house singing, but have never been able to learn to whistle. Inability to whistle is a general characteristic of passive inverts. I learned to sew and crochet, and naturally took to most other feminine lines of activity, so that my mother has remarked that I was "the best daughter" she had. Indeed none of the family looked upon me as a boy, all unconsciously. Nevertheless there is little evidence that any of them ever suspected that I was attracted toward the male sex.

As a child and youth I was rather odd even apart from my androgynism. For example, from my eleventh to my thirteenth year, while sitting at my desk or walking the streets alone, I would, without raising the head, direct my eyes upward for about two seconds at intervals of from five to ten minutes in order to breathe a short prayer for acquaintances or for pitiable looking individuals whom I passed. It was probably a sort of St. Vitus dance of the muscles about the eye. Another peculiar action, and one which I have never seen in any other person, is the lifelong craze that I have to press the flesh bordering the finger nails against some sharp hard corner, as that of a book-cover or a pillow-case, which repeated action renders the skin horny along the edge of the nail, so that I have often been able to peel it off.

From the age of nine to sixteen, my parents sent me to a large boys' private school. At first the experience was painful to me. I felt out of place, and would have preferred attending a girl's school, or at least a co-educational one. Through my school-life up to the age of fourteen, a sense of shame kept me from going to the lavatory except when the need was most urgent, and until the age named, I never sat down there. I never lingered on the play-ground, and mingled with the boys only in the class-room. I particularly avoided them when they were tossing a ball, being very much afraid it might roll near me, and I would have to throw it. The few times that this did happen, the boys laughed, because, they said, I threw just like a girl.

Through all my school life, I hardly had a rival in respect to high standing in all my studies. Near the close of my school career, I was proclaimed before the whole school by the principal as the model student, and the average of all my marks for the last four years of the course was the highest ever attained by any student at that school up to that time.

Between my eighth and my thirteenth year, I several times saw boys in solitary onanism. It gave me a violent desire facere id iis, and also for fellatio. But shame conquered, and I would not betray my desire to my nearest boy friend. For years I slept with an intensely masculine brother. Several times he requested fellatio, but even when in bed, I turned away in shame. Because he was my brother, I had never felt drawn until finally, about my thirteenth year, he committed solitary onanism before my eyes. From this time on, no sleep would come to my relief until I had followed out my instincts. After he fell asleep, I would simply labra mea peni ejus for one second. I never disturbed him enough to awaken him, or even to cause him to have an orgasm, except once, when he asked me to proceed, but for shame I would not. On the other nights, the mere contact for a second would induce a paroxysm. I immediately had the most dreadful sensation imaginable, so that the thought held complete possession of my being: "I'll never do it again! I'll never do it again!" I closed and unclosed my hands convulsively. My memory is that there was an emission, but not until two years later did I know the nature of the discharge. Immediately after the paroxysm I always fell asleep as if from exhaustion.

Thus my habit of early childhood was renewed after about five years continence. Up until past the age of forty, I believed that the early fellatio was without injurious effect on mind and body, but that that of my thirteenth year was decidedly baneful to both. After passing the age of forty, I am doubtful as to whether the indulgences at either period were injurious.

But happily the period of these thefts lasted probably less than six weeks. My parents possibly learned of it. Any way I was soon assigned a room and a bed all to myself, which I have continued to have down to the time when this autobiography goes to press. Subsequently, between my thirteenth and seventeenth years, emergency destined me to sleep only three times with a boy friend, when also instinct triumphed surreptitiously.

Beginning at the age of twelve and continuing two years, I could not sleep for approximately two hours after retiring. My thoughts were entirely of boys and of myself as a girl. I imagined all sorts of flirtations and amours with every decidedly good-looking boy with whom I went to school. I would sugere finger or plum or other similarly shaped object, and imagine it was the membrum virile first of one acquaintance, and then of another. I would imagine myself breaking into their houses after they had gone to bed, and attaining my desire. I would imagine a dozen of them standing behind a long screen, with erectis sticking through apertures, and myself going from one to another, according to instinct. I would imagine myself walking on a lonely road and meeting a handsome youth, a stranger, who would force me to fellatio. I would imagine boys keeping me a prisoner in a secluded place and compelling me every day to fellatio. I would imagine myself a beautiful girl skating in the rink, and having a bevy of boys frolicking with me—I falling down and having several of them pile on top of me. In many of these reveries, indeed, I imagined myself clad in feminine apparel. I also indulged in this kind of revery while taking long walks alone through the country. My present judgment on my entertaining such a current of thought is that I was for the most part irresponsible, and that these reveries were due to my being driven in a measure insane by the lack of any outlet for an innate excessive amorousness.

These reveries in bed were accompanied by an orgasm, but I never had any inclination toward solitary onanism. Though knowing the difference between male and female pudenda, I did not until later, about my fourteenth year as I remember, know their function, reproduction. As I lay abed, I would wish and pray that my pudenda might be changed to those of a girl, largely with the thought that I might be enabled to receive boys. I knew what went on between some boys and girls, but I did not know that anything ever resulted from the act. The fact that I was a boy—or rather that my body was that of a boy, because in mind I was thoroughly a girl—occasioned me an immense amount of regret and chagrin, and continued to do so down to the age of forty, as I approached which age, my sexual life was retreating more and more into the background, so that I became rather indifferent as to my physical and psychical sex.

I have been doomed to be a girl who must pass her earthly existence in a male body. How dreadful it is to a young woman to have a slight growth of hair on lip or cheeks! Only one mark of the male! How much more dreadful for a young woman to possess almost all the male anatomy as I do! How I have bewailed my fate! During my early teens, being in a frenzy sometimes over it, I would meditate taking my father's razor and castrating myself in order to bring my physical form more in accord with that of the female sex to which I instinctively yearned to belong.

Once during the wishes and prayers spoken of above, I reached my hand down and momentarily believed I had been miraculously provided with a cunnus. It is my present impression that my hand came in contact with the scrotum, and that it was my first perception that I had such an appendage. Possibly this indicates late descent of the testicles. As I remember it, up to about my thirteenth year, I never knew there was a scrotum on any male. All my intimates of early childhood had been fully dressed, and thus this organ was concealed.

Up to about my fourteenth year, I regarded fellatio as a wicked shameful habit which evil-minded children fell into, and the desire for which I would outgrow as I became older. From my fourteenth to my seventeenth year, I regarded it as the very worst kind of a habit, which must be overcome by a hard struggle. I had no idea the desire was to continue into and through my adult life.

Up to about my fourteenth year, I also thought normal coitus, which I knew some boys and girls of my acquaintance were guilty of, was equally heinous. When at about the age of thirteen I was told by boys that babies thus came into being, I at first refused to believe it. When I was finally convinced, it was with a realization that every member of the human race was as vile as myself. Subsequently, down to my middle twenties, I considered the subject of love between the sexes as one which should never be mentioned in polite society, a subject which ought to bring deep blushes to every cheek.

After the age of twelve, I no longer masqueraded in feminine apparel or openly flirted with boys because restrained by the sense of shame. Because all the lexicographers wrongly insist on the *feigned* character of flirtations, I am moved to explain here once for all that my flirtations, in every period of my life, were *sincere*, and prompted by adoration for those flirted with. The same explanation applies to my use of "coquet."

But while no longer openly and energetically flirting with boys, I still adored them, enjoyed their occasional petting attentions, and even sometimes put myself in the way of receiving such consideration. For a brief period during my fourteenth year, I used powder to make my cheeks more rosy with a view to impressing my schoolmates, with several of whom I was in love.

About the time of my learning the secret of reproduction, circumstances brought me one night to sleep with a boy friend, and my instincts prevailed while he slept. On this occasion the terrible paroxysm accompanying fellatio two years earlier, as already described, and putting an end to it almost before it had begun, was not experienced, and the act continued for some minutes. I did not yet know of the existence of semen, but believed the simple presence membrum virile in membro femineo induced pregnancy. Even if I had had an emission myself two years before, I knew absolutely nothing about its nature. For several months after this night's experience I was somewhat worried for fear of pregnancy, thinking it might result from buccal coitus.

During my early teens also, a few schoolmates hinted at fellatio. Because of shame I gave them no encouragement, although almost insane for love of them. Moreover, about this time, several old and middle-aged men would find occasion to clasp me, cum peni adversum fundamentum meum. They evidently entertained thoughts of paedicatio, but on account of our position in society, they did not go any farther. I abhorred their conduct.

As a consequence of my comparatively solitary life, my association with boys being confined to the school-room, I was very backward in acquiring normal sexual knowledge, never used slang, and was in general a "goody-goody." Other boys called me an "innocent." Adults regarded me as exceptionally guileless and pure-minded. The reader will discover in these pages what manner of person I was, but down to my middle thirties my "childlike and bland smile" and my "frank and open countenance" have been harped upon by my every-day associates. Down to the age named they have described me as "mild-eyed," "inoffensive," "childlike," and "lamblike."

I was probably more a prey to sensual imaginations than any other boy of the community, and yet, without any attempt to deceive on my part, I was judged to be the most pure-minded! Nevertheless, though naturally one of the most sensual, I probably practiced the most self-denial. Later, college associates remarked that they never met any one else with so little of the animal in him, when actually I was then perhaps the most given to venery of them all. I had in myself the germs of two as widely opposed careers as it would be possible to name. I was a born religious and philanthropic worker. On the other hand, no girl was ever more clearly cut out for the life of a fille de joie than was I.

The genitals became pubescent as early as the completion of my fifteenth year. Is this not unusually early for a male, but the proper age for a female? Whether or no as a partial effect of this beginning of pseudo-puberty, I simultaneously developed into a religious prodigy, leading the congregation in church in extempore prayer at this early age, and spending a full two hours daily in private religious exercises for the next two years. At this time I definitely chose the Christian ministry in a heathen land as my field of labor when I had finished my education. This greatly increased interest in religion fortunately put a stop to my morbid reveries. I now looked upon my yearning for fellatio as my "besetting sin," and until the age of nineteen fought against it as few others have struggled to be freed from lustful desires. A popular medical writer has described the girl-boy as "congenitally depraved," and "secretly vicious." I would refute this and other slanderers of the girl-boy, cursed by Nature and cursed by his fellow man. Lofty ethical ideals, including self-abnegation, are as common among youthful inverts as among those normally sexed.

From my fourteenth to my seventeenth year, I passed a rather sad and lonely life. I was ashamed longer to mingle with girls as one of them, and still shrunk from companionship with boys. My recreation consisted of long solitary walks through the country during which I brooded over the real and imagined ills of life. Being delicate, I hardly expected to live to reach manhood.

Erotic dreams, with emissions, began at the age of fifteen, and in a few months reached a frequency of twice a week. The fraudulent advertisements in the newspapers held out to me the strong probability of my soon becoming an idiot as a result of these losses, and occasioned me much despondency. Only males have figured in these dreams. They related only to fellatio, never to paedicatio.

It was during my seventeenth year that I first became fully conscious that my unwilling craving for fellatio was deeply rooted, and not to be outgrown; that my feeling for my schoolmates was the procreative instinct, in me misdirected. The realization that I was differently constituted from nearly all other males, and such an individual as during the whole history of the human race—so far as I was then acquainted with the history of the phenomenon—has been abhorred, reviled, and regarded as the lowest of the low, a monster of wickedness, and an outcast, was accompanied by the bitterest sorrow, causing me about once a week to go forth at night to a lonely quasi-abandoned graveyard, throw myself on the grass-covered graves, writhe in an agony of tears and moans, and beseech my Creator by a miracle then and there to take away my perverted instinct and make a virile man of me. These seasons of anguish would exhaust me mentally and physically for twenty-four hours afterward. This was the beginning of three such melancholy years as few are called to pass through, and I meditated suicide repeatedly.

For several months I bore my sorrow alone, shame preventing my making my spiritual adviser my confidant. I was at last driven to him for consolation, and on his advice, with the greatest shame and in broken language, made my secret known to my family physician. The latter advised me to enter into courtship with some girl acquaintance, and said that this would render me normal. Like most physicians in 1890, he did not understand the deepseated character of my perversion. Although it was counter to my inclinations, I cultivated the society of a girl friend. But after months of effort, feminine beauty proved powerless to attract me in the least, while male beauty was constantly increasing its sway over me.

In September of 1891 I entered a university in the City of New York, which was only an hour by train from my home. During the first two years I was regularly engaged in mission work in the slums as an avocation. I preached about twelve times from the pulpit, besides being the leader of about a hundred secondary church services.

Life in a great city soon made its impress on my constitutional femininity, which, for several years practically suppressed as a matter of conscience, was now calling louder and louder for expression. Moreover, in a great city, the temptation to a double life is exceptional. One can so easily hide a disgraceful act. It was especially unfortunate that I saw so much of the loose morals of the slums. The adolescents there attracted me powerfully, and suggestions came into my mind repeatedly to accost them with an indecent purpose.

I was also constantly in love with athletic classmates. In the lecture rooms I found it advisable to take a front seat since the sight of an athlete would hypnotize me, making me stare at his form and disregard the lecturer. If one seated himself beside me, shameful thoughts would come into my mind at once. While seated in the lecture room, some of them have put their arms around me and said "Child." They have taken my hand in theirs and said it was just like a girl's hand. When my sleeves were rolled up they have said that my arms were just like a girl's arms. Their laying their hands on me was ineffably sweet, and always occasioned an orgasm, but modesty forbade betraying my feminine feelings. None ever even hinted at anything further than what I have just narrated.

On my visits home during this first year in college, I was supersensitive to my family's criticism of me for lack of manliness. I sometimes felt like never visiting home again because of my shame at being an effeminate man. I shunned all social gatherings because I detested the idea of courting a female and putting myself forward as a man. I would nevertheless weep at seeing other young people enjoying the ordinary legitimate pleasures of love without my ever—as I then thought—being privileged to have a share in them, since love and courtship in my case must be with one of my own physical sex. I often wished I might get away from the world and live as a monk or, better in my own case, a hermit. Then I would be in a way unsexed, and would be so regarded by the world. As to be a monk one must be a Roman Catholic, I contemplated going over to that religious body.

One day I happened to be left alone in the room of an athletic classmate. I spent the whole time in passionately kissing his pillow and articles of clothing. Especially did corduroy braccas feel most exquisite labris as I osculated partem prope locum membri virilis. If he had not been fair to look upon and decidedly virile, it would have been nauseating even to *think* of doing what I did.

Afterward, repentant, I wrote in my journal: "Religion, reputation, life itself, ready to put all at stake for a few moments enjoyment! I never felt so much like a wretch as I do now! If only I had thought more of the love of Christ to me, I might not have so far yielded! For a month nearly all my reading has been of a religious character; I have for a month been in close communion with God; yet in a moment I can so fall away! O to understand more fully salvation from sin through Christ, and to experience more of it in my own life! . . . I feel this morning that I can never enter the ministry. I feel that I must give up all my plans, and that maybe I shall come to a miserable end."

All my life corduroy trousers and rubber boots have attracted me sexually more than any other articles of civilian dress. I have always considered both articles too masculine for me to wear. It would have filled me with shame to be seen wearing boots. At the age of ten I would go secretly to the closet where a brother's corduroy braccas hung and do as described above. On other occasions prior to my fifteenth year I have arisen at night and similarly osculated braccas puerorum who were our guests, creeping stealthily into their rooms in a highly excited state and trembling violently. On only two occasions I approached their bed and touched them, but did not dare go further for fear they would awake. I have no doubt now that I was irresponsible, and any girl-boys ever found guilty of similar conduct should be dealt with compassionately.

Speaking of fetishes,—from boyhood the military uniform has been a magnet. During my twenties the sight of it would bring on a sort of babyish and effeminate dance of various members of the body and a sort of pouting. It would rivet my gaze, I would halt and turn around as the soldier passed, and mark his every movement until he disappeared. I would consider his gait and his every sway and swagger as marvellously manly and in every way wonderful.

Of those under thirty years of age, nineteen out of twenty soldiers or sailors in uniform have captivated me, but hardly one out of twenty civilians. But I generally had to get used to the uniform. When the olive drab was first adopted for American soldiers, I had only disgust for

T he following was written in my diary about the middle of my freshman year:

"I sometimes think I am an irresponsible being. De Quincey is exonerated from censure for his opium habit. May God not also pardon my cherishing amorous thoughts of the kind peculiar to me—abnormal for others, yet for me normal? I am by nature very amorous, and have been all my life, even in infancy, when I could not distinguish between good and evil. Further, all my life I have been thrown in with what is to me the opposite sex—compelled to mingle and live with them. I had nothing to do with the bringing about of this peculiar nature and environment of mine. Has it been my fault that my amorous desires have run into the channel they have, the channel opened to them when I was in the state of innocence and ignorance of a three-year-old child? I am really a woman, and a very amorous one at that, although regarded as a man because the majority of my physical traits are those of the male sex. Did society ever compel any other woman, except those like me, to live, eat, sleep, frequent the same comfort-rooms and baths, lie sometimes in the same bed, with men, and sometimes to listen to the unclean talk of men? I am driven wild by instinctive cravings more than any other human being ever was. . .

"I wish I was not of an amorous nature. It makes my life miserable. If I had my choice, it would be a life entirely free from all sexual phenomena—complete sexual indifference. How gladly would I be free from all passion, so that I could make a name for myself in the world! My highest ideal is to be a Christian philosopher, and to preach the Gospel to those who are living in sin and sorrow. An amorous person can hardly be a philosopher, a scholar, and a preacher. . ."

Shortly afterward, in a letter to my family physician, I wrote as follows:

"I would like to know if you think there is any possibility of my ever following my instincts without sin? It is right for the normal individual to appease natural craving in wedlock. Is it not also right for me to do the same if the opportunity should offer? For instance, I will suppose an almost impossible case. If I should ever come across a young man whom I loved and who would marry me, would it be right for me to live with him as his wife? This supposition is probably highly repulsive to you, but absolutely, looking at it philosophically, it is no more unseemly and monstrous for me to be joined in wedlock with the man I would love above everything else in the world, than for a normal individual to enter into the state of matrimony.

"I long to be made the pet of my classmates. Would it be unbecoming to show my girlishness to them occasionally, and welcome and encourage their caresses which I sometimes receive? I still often pray God to deaden these desires to receive tokens of a reciprocated passion on the part of those whom I sexually worship, but I am beginning to add, 'If it be Thy will;' because maybe it is for my highest good and happiness to have these feelings toward my associates.

"I desire to know the mysteries of my peculiar life. It seems to me I have a right to know. I spent several days recently in ransacking the college library for the information I desire, but found almost nothing. If the science of medicine knows anything about my peculiarity, I demand of you to know it.

"Lately from a conversation of some students that I heard, I chanced to learn more about my peculiar affliction than I ever knew before. I heard brief accounts of four persons cursed as I am, 'With their procreative instincts centered in their heads instead of in the usual organs,' as one of the students expressed it. These four victims were all intellectual men; one, a young clergyman; one, an elderly judge; and two, principals of schools. They were found out by their communities. The clergyman committed suicide, and the others had to flee from the stern hand of the law. . .

"You thus see that I may some day have to flee from the wrath of men by suicide, or by self-imposed exile in a distant land, where I doubt if I could stand the misery I would suffer, forever removed from all my dear ones, and worse than dead to them. No one would have any mercy on me, and my name would be held up as that of a consummate hypocrite and the most degraded of men. But more than anything I would suffer, I would bring my parents in sorrow to the grave."

About this time I read the eminent theologian Lange's comments on St. Paul's teaching about marriage, and through these, as well as through my own deep reflections, I was becoming more than ever persuaded that since it was God who had planted these instincts in me at birth, they could not be so horribly sinful as I had been led to believe. Nevertheless I was not finally convinced. A month later I stayed up all of one night in order to reconsider the question, desiring and purposing to convince myself of the sinfulness of an invert's harboring the suggestions of instinct to the slightest degree. I weighed carefully all the passages of sacred scripture bearing on the case, and finally determined to fight harder than ever to annihilate in myself all the movings of the sexual nature. In the following weeks, I occasionally did not leave my room all day, fasting, praying, and studying the scriptures.

During this winter of '91–'92, paroxysms of melancholia occasionally came upon me at night. When I felt their approach, I could not stand it to remain in my room, where I must be noiseless, but went out to a deserted spot in a large park near which I lived, where I would shriek repeatedly. All my muscles seemed to be rigid, and my fists were clinched. I would dig my finger-nails into my palms, and wave my arms wildly. Within a few minutes, my strength would be completely gone. I looked upon these paroxysms as fits of insanity, and feared I would become permanently and violently insane. I now attribute these attacks largely to unsatisfied, involuntary yearnings for the mate which Nature had designed me to have. If society had permitted me one, and I had been taught that it was right for me to have one, I would have been saved an enormous amount of suffering, as well as perhaps my subsequent career as a fairie.

About the middle of April came a characteristic experience of an invert's life. Shortly before my usual hour of retiring, an old schoolmate, a stalwart and handsome youth, who had spent the day in the city, called and asked to remain over night. I experienced a shock, knowing the temptation such an arrangement would be to me. For several weeks I had been living a life almost free from amorous thoughts, due to the lengthened seasons of religious exercises spoken of above.

Out of considerations of hospitality, I could not but grant my friend's request. How could I bring myself to explain to him that I was essentially a girl, and so our spending a night in the same room was not to be thought of? I inquired if there was not a vacant room in the house, but that night there was none. Of course I could have given up my room and gone to a hotel, but I had to be saving, and such a course would humiliate my friend. So I arranged for him to occupy my bed, and for myself to sleep on the floor. Sleeping alone on the floor, I felt strong enough to resist, as I had done before when forced to sleep in the same room with a youth to whom I was attracted, and I would have probably resisted on the present occasion if it had not been for an unusual and unforeseen incident which inflamed me as never before.

My guest was moderately addicted to sensuality. As we were about to retire, he handed me, without evil intentions, a libidinous rhyme to read, the first I had ever seen. I became intoxicated, and my companion happening to absent himself from the room for a few moments, I passionately osculated the paper the rhyme was written upon. My fleshly nature immediately determined to have its desire that night, but my spiritual nature counselled otherwise. It was to be a struggle of hours. "Self-praise goes but little ways," but I believe that there are comparatively few of the human race who, with a nature peculiarly susceptible to sensuality, as mine was, would have resisted as long as I did the force of so many evil suggestions.

After retiring, the young man soon slept. But I was unable to sleep, no matter how hard I tried. My mind was unusually active. I continually prayed that sleep might come and save me from yielding, because I felt that my own poor will could not resist the long pent-up force of passion. Notwithstanding all my prayers, nothing was further from me that night than sleep.

It was a night following a Sabbath spent in communion with God, and with a strong determination to live a life of self-abnegation for the sake of others. But through the long hours of wakefulness, the influence of the sexual nature grew stronger and stronger. For hours I vacillated between cherishing the suggestions of the spiritual nature and those of the flesh. My chief defence against the latter was the thought that if I yielded this once, I must from now on give up all idea of ever becoming a preacher of the Gospel.

Moreover, the young man knew I was engaged in religious work, and expected to enter the ministry, and what would he henceforth think of the genuineness and utility of religion? If it had not been for my occupying an active position in religious work and my looking forward to entering the Christian ministry, I would have yielded much sooner on the present occasion, as well as indulged my instincts much earlier in my career.

As I grew more and more weary mentally and physically, I naturally grew weaker and weaker in will power. The seducer of souls finally conquered. I suddenly found myself lying on the foot of my guest's bed. The transition seemed to have taken place in a moment of unconsciousness. Being exhausted, I had probably dozed off for a moment, walked there in my sleep, and again fully waked up as I laid myself on the bed. As the Ruth of the scriptures—but I wish to emphasize it, without premeditation and unconsciously—I had come softly, uncovered the young man's feet, and lain down. Before long he awoke, and heartily acquiesced in my desires. For fellatio, I at the moment felt ready to forsake all plans for leading a useful and respected life—for I thought it meant that.

The next morning I was ashamed to look my guest in the face, and stammered forth an apology. I was really irresponsible for my conduct, but at the time believed I had wilfully sinned, and when the time of temptation was past, sincerely repented. In my diary I wrote:

"What harm may I not have brought on Christ's cause by my recent action! I may have endangered the eternal welfare of my friend. I suppose he thinks I am a nice one to be thinking of becoming a minister of the Gospel. I feel ashamed to make any further profession of religion before him. O to be holy and pure! I think I am holy enough to be a clergyman if it were not for my sins arising from my abnormal passion. . .

"Miserable wretch, miserable wretch, miserable wretch, that's all I am! I am ashamed to look any one in the face any more. I feel very much like putting an end to my life, or else going off to some place where none of my friends will know I am. I wish this morning to die speedily, to be killed in an accident on the street. I would like just now to lay down my life for others. I have nothing to live for. I am one of the unhappiest of mortals. I may be disgraced, disgrace my family, bring reproach upon the cause of Christ, be compelled to flee, be disowned by my parents, be cursed and be despised throughout the land. I will flog myself and starve myself, to see if I cannot conquer my body.

"Because of my many failures to follow Christ perfectly in the past, and because something out of the ordinary is necessary to root out my procreative instincts, I now vow before God to imitate the example of Christ, who spent much time alone in meditation and prayer, and to spend hereafter one hour every morning and one hour every evening in the study of God's word, in meditation, and in prayer."

For some weeks I fulfilled this vow. But my seasons of devotion gradually became less and less edifying, and at last I reached the point where the spirit of prayer—that is, of conversation and communion with the Great Omnipresent Spirit—left me entirely, and the words of sacred scripture, formerly falling upon my eyes and mind with a strange power and revealing to me, and enabling me to live, the larger, heavenly, eternal life, where sensuality has disappeared, were now read mechanically and failed to impress me except as being tedious.

Sensual thoughts now began to creep into my mind more and more. Interest in my studies was declining. In the class-room I was absent-minded, and when called upon, would be confused, and hardly able to reply to the professor's questions. Even here I would be thinking of the soft satin-smooth cutis in inguine of my late guest which I had found gratissima tactioni, praesertim labiali et linguali, and would regret that it was always to be denied to me to touch again on viro this marvellously fine integument. I pined for the repetition of other similar pleasures which I had for the first time tasted in their fulness only a few weeks before, such as pillowing caput super abdomene aut femure nudo adolescentis, the fascinating sight membri virilis ejus erecti, and the extremely smooth surface glandis, gratissima tactioni et digitorum et oris.

While walking the street, my gaze would be riveted on stalwart adolescents, and I would halt to look back at the handsomest that passed. If a street-car conductor happened to be youthful and good-looking, I became almost irrational. With a look of despair I would gaze insolently and imploringly into the face of the blueclad youth as if I would compel him to read my thoughts, since I did not dare give them expression. When in a crowded car he brushed against me in passing, a tremor would pass over my body. Youthful policemen also at this time particularly fascinated me. Blue clothing and brass buttons have always made a young man appear to me as at his best.

After retiring at night, my unwilling desire to be in amplexu adolescentis did not permit me to sleep. Through long hours of wakefulness I writhed on my bed and repeatedly groaned in despair. "Am I being tried by fire?" I would ask myself. "'For every one will be salted with fire,' says the scripture. Are others so tried by fire as I have been through a large part of my life? Maybe this is what God is doing to me in implanting the strongest of desires and then forbidding my gratifying them."

Even in the midst of almost continuous prayer, my delirious imagination brought before me obscene images, which I repeatedly tried in vain to expel from my mind. Several times during the struggle I would rise and walk up and down the room for a few moments. After retiring for perhaps the third or fourth time, I would rise once more, go raving about the room like an insane person, and if it had not been for the lateness of the hour, about midnight, I would have gone out in search of fellatio, which could alone pacify me. I was at last able to fall asleep only by making the resolution to undertake the search on the following evening. But on several evenings I postponed it because of the overwhelming dread of setting out, as well as because the desire was not so insistent until it became time to go to bed.

During these terrible days, I felt that a crisis in my life was at hand. I felt that I stood at the dividing of the ways, one leading to honor and self-approbation the other to ignominy and the blasting of all my legitimate ambitions. As each month of my first year in the university went by, the struggle against sensuality had been growing harder and harder.

Finally, on an evening in early June, I arose from my studies and prepared for my first nocturnal ramble. I put on a cast-off suit which I kept for wear only in my room, placed some coin in a pocket and several bills in a shoe, stuffed a few matches in one pocket and in another a wet sponge, wrapped in paper so as not to dry out, and then carefully went through my clothing a second time to make sure that I had not by oversight left on me some clue to my identity.

On account of my shabby clothing, precaution was necessary to leave my place of residence—a high-class boarding-house—without being seen. I crept stealthily out of my room, closing the door softly so as not to attract attention. After listening to make sure that no one was about to ascend the outside steps leading to the street, I opened the outer door and glided out bare-headed, a cast-off soft cap crumpled up in my hand because I was ashamed to be seen wearing it by any one who knew me. Hurriedly crossing to the opposite side of the street, I put on the cap, pulling the tip down over my eyes. Walking a few blocks to a park, I took my house key from my pocket and hid it in the grass, so that it could not be stolen and I thereby rendered unable to let myself in on my return.

The reader now beholds me for the first time transformed into a sort of secondary personality inhabiting the same corpus as my proper self, to which personality I soon gave the name of "Jennie June," and which personality was to become far more widely known in the immediately following dozen years than the other side of my dual nature, the unremitting student and scholar, was ever to be known. The feminine side of my dual nature, for many years, as a matter of conscience, repressed, was now to find full expression in "Jennie June." For it was not alone fellatio that I craved, but also to be looked upon and treated as a member of the gentler sex. Nothing would have pleased me more than to adopt feminine attire on this and my multitudinous subsequent female-impersonation sprees, as some other ordinarily respectable androgynes are in the habit of doing when going out on similar promenades, but my position in the social organism was much higher than theirs, and the adoption of female apparel would in my case have been attended with too great risk. The mere wearing of it on the street by an adult male would render him liable to imprisonment.

I made my way to the quarter of the city bordering the Hudson River that is given over largely to factories and freight yards and is known as "Hell's Kitchen" because of the many steam vents. In this lonely and at night little frequented neighborhood, perhaps the most advantageous in the city for highway robbery, where nothing else than burning passion could have induced me to go at night, I ran across a stalwart adolescent of about my own age seated alone on a beer keg in front of a bar room. By a great effort of the will I accosted him. My voice trembled and my whole body shook as if I had the ague.

I had anticipated little difficulty in securing a companion, but events showed it to be otherwise. For years subsequently I associated intimately with hundreds of unmarried toughs of the slums from seventeen to twenty-four years of age, and so I know their nature. Approximately one-third have a distaste for coitus with an invert. The other two-thirds would accommodate him provided their sexual needs were not fully met by normal intercourse—which is generally the case. Moreover, there is a difference between their attitude toward a perfect stranger who accosts them, and an invert with whom they have become somewhat acquainted. The impulse to rob a perfect stranger tends to drown out all the movings of carnality. In addition, the feeling that he is a stranger and an outlaw—the latter fact being almost universally known—prompts them to assault him.

Along with an outline of what happened on this my first nocturnal ramble, I describe below my general method of approaching strangers in the poor quarters of the city. Of course I cannot recall the exact dialogue in a particular case, but all the sample conversations given in this autobiography are woven from *actual* remarks passed at different times. I have taken part in hundreds of dialogues of the kind sampled here and there in this book, and the reader can be assured of obtaining a truthful impression of the words exchanged by me—an androgyne— with my youthful virile associates. On the present occasion, after a few commonplace remarks, the conversation was of the following character:

"What big, big strong hands you have! I bet you are a good fighter." My aim was to talk rather babyishly so as gradually to betray my nature.

"There's a few as kin lick me but not many."

"I love fighters. If you and I had a fight, who do you think would win?"

"I could lick a dozen like yer together."

"I know you could. I am only a baby."

"Hah hah! A baby!"

"Say, you have a handsome face."

"Me hansome! Stop your kiddin."

"Really you are handsome. I am going to tell you a secret. I am a woman-hater. I am really a girl in a fellow's clothes. I would like to get some fellow to marry me. You look beautiful to me. Would you be willing to?"

"How much does it cost yer to git married? Give me a V (meaning five dollars) and I'll be yourn, or else git out of here."

My statement that I had not that amount with me brought the threat of a pummeling. I was beginning to wish I was far away, but concealed my uneasiness as best I could. After a few minutes more of conversation, several pals happened to come along. He called out, "I've got a fairie here!" and clutching my shoulder with one hand, he clinched his other fist, shook it threateningly in my face, and demanded: "Hand out your money! Hand out your money!"

Frightened to death, I handed him all the coin I had, amounting to a little more than a dollar. I protested I had no more, and after they had searched my pockets and felt my clothing all over for concealed bills, one of them gave me a blow in the face. With that wonderful agility which supposedly grave danger to one's life can arouse, I sprinted away, one of the ruffians pursuing a few steps and giving me several blows in the back. But I was so terrified that I did not halt until I had run several blocks. Panting and exhausted, I seated myself on a door-step and felt that I was forever cured of seeking a paramour. I called to mind the biblical text, "The way of the transgressor is hard," and I felt glad that it was hard so as to help me never to transgress again.

But after I had rested, my intense desire for fellatio induced me to make an endeavor in another poor neighborhood. I passed many groups of ruffians congregated in front of bar-rooms, but must find some solitary adolescent. At last I ran across one standing in front of a factory, evidently, as I later concluded, its watchman. I walked past him several times, unable to pluck up courage to speak. But he called out angrily: "Who are you looking at?"

"Pardon me for my rudeness, but I was wishing I could get acquainted with you. I am a baby, and I want a big, strong, brave fellow like you to pet me. I'll give you a dollar if you'll pet me for a few minutes, and let me sit on your lap."

Much to my surprise and disappointment, he sent me away with a curse. Twice repulsed, I decided to try again in a part of the city where the immigrant element predominates. Both the neighborhoods tried were quasi-American. I strolled down the Bowery, staring longingly and beseechingly into the eyes of the adolescents I passed, but too timid to accost any. Those who had known me all my life, had they met me now, would have wondered what could have brought into the then theatre and red-light district of the foreign laboring classes of the city, at an hour approaching midnight, a timid youth, hitherto called an "innocent," naturally pious, and generally esteemed for his intellectual tastes. My friends would never have dreamed that I would frequent that red-light district near midnight, and would never have believed it if any one told them that I was there for no good purpose.

Arrived at the southern end of the Bowery, I turned into New Bowery, because it looked dark and crime-inviting. I roamed for another half-hour in the dark, deserted streets of this quarter, accosting one or two young dockrats who were still abroad, but they simply ransacked my pockets, gave me a parting blow, and went on their way. Moistening my handkerchief at a drinking fountain, I washed my bloodstained face. Finally, after midnight, thoroughly sobered by my disappointments and physical smarting, I boarded a car. Securing my key from its hiding place, I let myself into my lodgings without any one ever learning of my nocturnal ramble.

How shall such conduct on the part of one of the members of an intellectual and decent community be judged? Let not the reader in pharasaical self-complacency—an attitude of mind all too common in dealing with the victims of congenital defects of mind or brain—begin to set his own virtue over against the apparent depravity of such as I. If he has not fallen as low as I, it is not necessarily because he is morally good, and I morally bad, but because in him there has been no overpowering impulse to do what mankind regards as unspeakably low. As to yielding to the sexual instinct, many have comparatively weak impulses in that direction, and could remain celibate all their lives without experiencing any kind or degree of suffering. Others would be rendered semi-mad by such abstinence, as was the case with me. The Rev. Robert Collyer has stated the matter well. It is like two young men to each of whom is given a field to cultivate. That of the one is fertile, free from stones, thicket, and weeds; that of the other a dense marshy jungle. Can the two contestants be expected in the same time to produce equally good crops of grain from their widely different pieces of land? Some men are born with much in their mental make-up that disposes them to evil, while others find it no effort to live virtuous lives.

While I have thus in my more mature judgment considered myself practically irresponsible for the conduct just described, in that early stage of my career, I was not so sure, and during the day following this first nocturnal ramble, was overwhelmed with a sense of shame and guilt. When night came on, I made my way to a solitary spot in a large park, where I threw myself on the ground to weep and shriek and pray. The burden of my prayer was that God would change my nature that very moment and give me the mind and powers of a man. I soon heard footsteps approaching, arose instantly, and walked from the spot. The men said they were looking for an owl which they had heard hooting. It was probably only my peculiar insane, half-suppressed shrieks they had heard.

At this time I entered the following in my diary: "I am experiencing the enslaving power of sin. I now know how to sympathize with poor sinners, drunkards and harlots. . . Do such perverse passions spring from idolatry and forgetting God, as St. Paul says? But for several years I have lived in communion with God. Several different times in my life I have passed a month without conscious sin. How can this accord with the fact that I have repeatedly in childhood and several times in youth committed the act (fellatio) recognized by men as the most heinous of crimes?"

I soon went to my village home for the summer, where I found the struggle against sensuality much less severe. For the first month there I lived without conscious sin. Through occupying my mind diligently with the high ethical ideals presented in the New Testament, and living continually in the spirit of prayer, I was able to bar completely from my life all the movings of the sensual nature, and all regard for self. Indeed I lived in this state of "entire sanctification" almost throughout the summer vacation, spending several hours a day in religious exercises. I came into intimate relations with a Christian faithcurist, and felt it to be my religious duty to be anointed by him for the removal of my perverted nature and for the reception of the normal instincts of a man. For over a month after the anointing, I persisted in the confident belief that God had miraculously brought about the change desired, and that I was now in full possession of the powers of a man. But gradually I had to admit the truth that no change had taken place.

My return to college in the fall of 1892 was followed by a decline from the high spiritual level attained during the summer vacation, this decline being especially marked by periods of depression, during which I would lament to myself that I was practically, by birth, an outcast from society, with a deformed nature, and despicable in the eyes of all people. I felt that I was a soft effeminate man who was wanted nowhere. At the sight of other young men rejoicing in their manly vigor, I would exclaim, "I want to die! I want to die!"

Moreover, possible ways of gratifying my sensual desires began to haunt me. Occasionally while walking the streets, I was powerfully constrained to embrace every young ruffian I met. I felt that I would gladly give up everything else in order to pass the rest of my days in the worst slums of the city in the company of the most vicious and degraded of mankind. At the same time I often had to sob violently while walking the streets when I would have a mental vision of myself given up to a life of shame in the slums, after having abandoned all my family ties in order to give free rein to my carnal desires. Sometimes I raved and wept like a mad man, and again I feared I might become completely insane.

About this time I came across two articles in a journal of anthropology which treated of eunuchs. I read that there is a class of abnormal human beings in India who are called "eunuchs by birth." The description given of their natures suited mine exactly. Though male in body—as stated in the article—they are feminine in manners and tastes, always wear women's clothes, let their hair grow long, and keep themselves clean shaven. They are filles de joie, and are happy in their lot. I now recalled that Bayard Taylor and other travellers in the east vaguely refer to them in their books. Not until now did I know the meaning of these references.

I now read also that males with such non-masculine and non-virile natures are found among the tribes of American Indians, by whom— according to the author I read—they are called "squaw-men." At a certain age, all the young males are called upon to choose between the weapons of the warrior and the staff of the squaw. These non-masculine males always choose the latter and are thenceforth looked upon as squaws, adopting the dress and occupations of the squaw, and becoming married to a brave. The hair that grows on their faces is plucked out as soon as long enough to get hold of.

I read further that such a class of males were found among the ancient Greeks, and recognized in their true character as not belonging to the warrior and ruling sex. I now recalled that my Greek professor had recently remarked that Phaedo had been a slave "devoted to unmentionable uses."

The immediate effect of this greatly increased self-knowledge was one of my most violent fits of weeping. I felt that there was nothing which could henceforth give me interest in life. I felt so mortified at thinking that I was a "man-woman," as such people are called in India. At this time I wrote in my diary: "People see that I am an effeminate man! an effeminate man! And one of my sisters remarked the last time I was home that she did not like effeminate men! Who can like them? Oh it looks as if there were no God in the world!"

If the reader had been on Mulberry Street between Grand and Broome on an evening in November of 1892, he would have seen meandering slowly along from one side of the street to the other with a mincing gait, a haggard, tired-looking, short and slender youth between eighteen and nineteen, clad in shabby clothes, and with a skull cap on his head. As he walks along, whenever he meets any robust, well-built young man of about his own age, who is alone, he is seen to stop and address to him a few words. If we had been able to follow this queer-acting individual for the previous hour before he passed us on Mulberry street, we would have seen him roaming about through all the streets of the then dark and criminal 4th Ward, occasionally halting near the groups of ruffians congregated in front of the bar-rooms, and then failing of courage to speak, pass along.

Finally on the corner of Broome and Mulberry Streets, he addresses a tall, muscular, splendid specimen of the adolescent (subsequently a member of the New York police force) who continues in conversation with him, and walks along by his side. The little adolescent takes the arm of the big one into his own, and presses as closely as possible against him. The spirits of the little one are visibly heightened, he appears more lively and animated, and walks along with a quicker but extremely nervous step. He is soon seized with a sort of ague—due to sexual excitement—which causes his whole body to shake, and hardly permits him to speak. If we watched closely whenever the pair passed under a shadow, we would have seen the little one throw his arms rapturously around the neck of his big companion, and kiss him passionately. They finally pass out of sight down one of the dark covered alleys leading to tenements in the rear.

When after an interval the pair again emerge, the smaller is clinging tighter than ever to his big companion, as if afraid he might escape. They walk a block together, and then the big fellow tries to get rid of the little one, much against the latter's wishes. He tells the little fellow to go on his way, but adds, "Come round again, do yer hear?"

"I don't know whether I shall or not. I am afraid we shall never meet again. How it pains me to part from you!"

"What do yer call yourself, and where do yer hang out?"

"I call myself Jennie, and I work in a restaurant up on Third Avenue. What's your name, and where could I find you again?"

"You kin find me round on this block any time. Just ask any one fur Red Mike."

"Well, good-by. The Lord bless you. I never expect to see you again, although I love you with all my heart, and would like to live with you and be your slave."

The two start off in opposite directions. The little fellow walks rapidly, turns the first corner, sprints, turns another corner and sprints, and repeats this maneuver several times, as if bent on giving the slip to any possible follower. He finally reaches the Bowery and takes a train uptown from the Grand Street station.

For several days following I suffered from shame and remorse. In order, if possible, to be cured of my abnormality, I now resolved to consult a specialist in venereal diseases, because at that time I believed my ailment came under that head. I was led to go to Dr. Prince A. Morrow, then the leading specialist in that line in New York City, who declared that either castration or marriage would be a sure cure for my abnormal passion! How many inverts have followed such advice of a physician, and seeking a cure in marriage, have been plunged into insanity or suicide, either on the eve of marriage, or soon after! Individuals like myself are women mentally. How is one woman to marry another, unless indeed one of the pair be a gynander, when marriage *de facto* often takes place. I could never think of tying myself to a wife until I felt myself to be a man.

Not satisfied, I immediately consulted another medical-college professor, this time an alienist, Dr. Robert S. Newton. Both drugs and electrical stimulation of the brain and spinal cord were tried. Hypnotism was attempted unsuccessfully. During the first month of treatment, I excluded from my mind all thoughts of sexual admiration. Then, though I continued to struggle against them, they would occasionally be present in the stream of thought for a few days, when with a fresh dedication of myself to God and to a life of self-renunciation, I would again completely banish them for another half-month.

After several months treatment, I was rendered almost a physical and nervous wreck by the powerful drugs administered, but my amorous desires showed no change. I now repeatedly appealed for castration. I argued that Nature had designed me to be a fille de joie—the worst fate possible as I then believed—and that castration alone could save me from it. But the answer was that I might in later years regret such a measure. I had recently read in a medical journal of a man similarly but not identically afflicted who was placed in possession of the normal procreative instinct through castration. During these months I had made diligent search at the library of the New York Academy of Medicine for light on my abnormality, and discovered a number of articles in American and foreign journals bearing on it.

During this course of treatment occurred one of the crises of my life. I had been appointed a delegate to a student's missionary convention in another city, and was assigned to a room with a rather athletic student from another college. The first night, after he had fallen asleep, I left the bed and lay on the floor, but was driven back by the cold. All possible alternatives were out of the question. Previous to that day, I had not known how I would have to pass the night. The chances were good that I would be assigned to a room alone, or else have an unattractive bed-fellow inasmuch as nine out of ten religious and studious adolescents were sexually repulsive, although highly esteemed as friends. Possibly I was cold to them because I myself am of a religious and studious disposition, as well as deficient in physical stamina, as they also are inclined to be.

I lay awake the whole night, but during the last half was in a sort of delirium. I partially yielded. The next morning, before several other students, my bed-fellow spoke sarcastically of me, evidently intending to visit on me what he considered to be deserved punishment. I was crushed by reason of shame, and they never saw me again, as I left by the next train. At the time I wrote in my diary:

"What have I ever done that God should make me suffer so? I feel that my abnormality bars me out of the ministry, the profession of my choice, and most likely out of all other professions. I feel that this passion is going to wreck my life, and never permit me to make any return to my parents for all they have done for me. I have no hope for the future. In the convention, while I would be singing, I was in thought hacking my body to pieces with a sword, or piercing my breast with a dagger. My continuous prayer was:

'Father, Father, hear my humble cry,
While on others thou art smiling,
Do not pass me by!'

"The convention, to me, was a lesson in resignation. The other young men were divinely brought there to be inspired with the Holy Spirit, to be instructed in regard to missionary fields and methods, to be called to preach the Gospel among those who sit in darkness; but I was brought there to learn the lesson of resignation in affliction, to experience the crushing to the earth by the mighty hand of God, to be tried like Isaac to see whether I am willing to be morally slain in my youth in a way which seems inexplicable. I have been preparing myself to become a foreign missionary, having had this career in mind from childhood; but God and Nature have undoubtedly destined me to be a (fille de joie). When a child of nine or ten years, although I had not learned that there were in the world such persons as fallen women, I often aspired to be a young woman, and to be a fallen one at that. I have resisted my fate with all the powers of my will and of my religious nature, but you cannot dam Niagara."

Not long afterwards I wrote: "Two ways open before me: one of sensual gratification, unrighteousness, falsehood, hypocrisy, dishonor; the other of blessing to the poor and the afflicted, a life which is holy and worthy of the good name given to it, a life which promises to my dear ones, on my account, more of health, happiness, and honor."

Shortly after writing the above, I brought the course of medical treatment to an abrupt termination. I would have continued longer if I had shown any improvement. I had lost all faith in the physician's ability to benefit me. Seeing that the science of medicine held out no hope, I felt more than ever that I was irresponsible for my abnormal sexual nature.

Over five months after my previous visit, I again found myself on Mulberry Street, corner of Grand. I have always suspected that I was incited to this particular quest by an aphrodisiac. On or about that day, my physician administered a new drug. He probably hoped it would incite me to seek normal relations, but it acted along the line of my peculiar instincts.

Walking northward on the west side of the street, I encountered a mixed group of Italian and Irish "sports" of foreign parentage between sixteen and twenty-one years of age seated or standing around the portal of a warehouse. I timidly addressed them: "I am looking for a friend named Red Mike. Do any of you know him?"

One of them replied that he had just seen him up the street. Proceeding in that direction, I stopped occasionally to make the same inquiry of other adolescents. After walking several blocks in vain, I returned to the "gang" at the warehouse's portal, and asked: "Do you mind if I sit down to rest here? I am tired and lonesome. I have not been in the city long and don't know any one."

"Where did yez come from?"

"Philadelphia. I couldn't get any work there, so I came here."

It was not long before Red Mike happened to stroll by and recognized me even before I did him. An hour now passed, while they smoked and drank, hiding the beer-pail whenever a policeman went by. I had no desire to join in the drinking and smoking, and indeed up to my middle forties, when this autobiography goes to press, have never had any desire to learn to smoke, although having a few times put the lighted cigarette of a paramour in my mouth. I have always considered myself too feminine to smoke. Moreover, all my life I have been practically a total abstainer from alcoholic beverages.

But I reclined in the arms of one after another, covering face, neck, hands, arms, and clothing with kisses, while they caressed me and called me pet-names. I was supremely happy. For the first time in my life I learned about the fairie inmates of the lowest dives. They proposed to install me in one. I told them the story of my own life, only with such variations from the truth as were necessary for my own protection. We sang plantation songs, "Old Black Joe," "Uncle Ned," etc. These they had learned from Bixby's "Home Songs," published in that very neighborhood by the well-known shoe-blacking firm as an advertisement. I sang with them in the mock soprano or falsetto that fairies employ, trying to imitate the voice of a woman. Singing in this voice was not a novelty to me, as I had previously at times aped the warbling of a woman instinctively.

At the end of an hour, we adjourned down an alley, where the drinking and love-making continued even more intensely. After I had refused their repeated solicitations, one of them grasped my throat tightly to prevent any outcry and threw me down, while another removed part of my clothing, appropriating whatever of value he found in my pockets. With my face in the dust, and half-suffocated by the one ruffian's tight grip on my throat, I moaned and struggled with all my might, because of the excruciating pain. But in their single thought to experience an animal pleasure, they did not heed my moans and broken entreaties to spare me the suffering they were inflicting. For two months afterward I suffered pain at every step because of fissures and lacerations about the anus.

When finally released, terror-stricken and with only half my clothing, I rushed out through the alley and down Mulberry Street, and did not halt until I reached what I considered a safe refuge on brightly lighted Grand Street. Breathless and exhausted, I seated myself on the curb. "I am cured of my slumming," I said to myself. "God's will be done. It is His hand which has brought this about, in order to drive me back to the path of virtue. Truly the Lord ruleth in all things."

Because of my exhausted condition, I remained seated for several minutes. In the meantime, two of my assailants had followed me up, and expressed their regret that one of their number had stolen my cap and coat, promising to get them back, and assuring me of their friendly feelings. "You are only a baby," they said, "and so we will fight for you and protect you."

I was so touched by their gallantry, so enamoured of them, and so sure that the assault was not committed through malevolence, that I accompanied them back to our first meeting place on the warehouse steps. I still had great fear of violence at their hands—rape, not a beating—but I was powerfully drawn toward them. Fellatio was welcome; paedicatio, horrible to my moral sense, and physically, accompanied by excruciating pain. The "gang" received me kindly, petted and soothed me as one would a peevish baby, which I resembled in my actions, fretting and sobbing in happiness as I rested my head against their bodies. To lie in the bosom of these sturdy young manual laborers, all of whom were goodlooking and approximately my own age, was the highest earthly happiness I had yet tasted. With all my money gone, and cap and coat stolen besides, I finally had to walk home, a distance of several miles. Obtaining my keys in their hiding place, I succeeded in reaching my room without attracting attention.

The next day I wrote in my journal: "What a strange thing is life! Mephistopheles last night carried me through one of the experiences through which he carried Faust. . . My carnal nature was aroused as never before. I groaned in despair. Never before in all my experience have I seen such a conflict between the flesh and the spirit. . . How like an animal is man! Thus God has seen fit to make him."

A few days later I again wrote: "My present psychical state is most strange. I cannot yet repent of my conduct last Friday night, yet on the Sunday following I had one of the happiest experiences of nearness to God that I ever had. That afternoon I presented the Gospel in love for my Savior and for perishing souls. I have in my heart an intense desire to save from their lives of sin those in whose company I was Friday night, especially my Bill, so young, and yet so deep in sin. I want to rescue him, and make of him a strong educated champion for Christ. My heart yearns to carry blessings and peace to all those who are suffering in the slums of New York."

In a letter received shortly afterward from a venerable doctor of divinity and former pastor, whom for years I made my confidant, he expressed his judgment of my conduct as follows: "I believe God will overlook in you what He would not in others."

The judgment of the alienist, to whom also I confided the occurrences, was approximately as follows: "It was a physical impossibility for you to have withstood longer. The only thing for you to do is to follow out your instincts in moderation. If you do not, you will continue to be a nervous wreck, and may even become insane. The majority of men can live celibate lives without suffering in mind or body, but you are extraordinarily amorous, and celibacy with you is out of the question. Only don't go into the slums any more. Confide in some stalwart young man of your own class. You run great risk of being killed, or at least contracting disease, in running around after strangers in the slums."

On now making my decision henceforth to follow Nature's behests, I gave up the city mission work I was engaged in, and also finally gave up my purpose of entering the Christian ministry. The presentation of religious truths spoken of above, on the Sunday following my third nocturnal ramble, was unavoidable, unless I wished to disappoint others by failing to keep an engagement. I gave up religious work, not because of lack of religious faith, but because I felt myself unworthy and unfit by reason of my recent change in habits, and because I might bring reproach on the Church.

I could not bring myself to follow the physician's advice to confide in a stalwart young man of my own class. I felt too much ashamed of my abnormality. So I formed the habit of visiting my Mulberry Street friends once a week, the visits continuing altogether for about a year. I preferred the society of these adolescent roughs to that of all other human beings, and woe to the friend of my ordinary circle who should hinder or delay me on the evenings on which I had planned a visit to Mulberry Street! If necessary to get rid of him, I would even insult any friend who happened to call at this inopportune time. At first exceedingly nervous for fear something would interfere with my setting out, I became, when safe from interruption after I had boarded the elevated train, blissfully intoxicated at the thought of meeting my beaux again.

During this period of living one evening a week according to the dictates of my peculiar instincts, I was happier than I had ever been before, notwithstanding my suffering for the first two months from a continuously painful sphincter ani. Recognizing the horror I had for paedicatio, and not wishing to drive me away from their "gang," particularly as my visits made them on those evenings what they regarded as flush with money, none ever again subjected me to it. But the lacerations of the first night required two months for healing. Moreover, I was never again robbed of my clothing.

The contrast in my own life between total abstinence and indulgence one evening a week was that the latter made me sing continually on the proper occasions, whereas with abstinence, I had been as continually weeping and moaning. I felt that I had come into possession of the earthly *summum bonum*, hitherto denied me. I had arrived at the conviction that while the voice of the world would cry "Shame!" I was acting according to the dictates of reason and conscience, and not sinning against the Holy Spirit. Nevertheless this conviction was occasionally shaken and I would be plunged into short spells of melancholia due to remorse over my sensual practices.

My favorite was an American-born Irish lad of nineteen, since he was both the handsomest and the most athletic. Because he soon became my "husband" *par excellence*, I foolishly thought I did wrong to deceive him as to my identity, as I did those who were not so closely related to me. But before I revealed the facts, I submitted the following declaration to be sworn to on a Bible:

"Do you solemnly swear that you will always keep inviolably secret my name, residence, our relations, and all that I confide to you, not revealing any of these things to your friends and pals without my permission?"

Although strongly urged, he refused to be sworn. He did not intend to keep what he was about to promise, and so was willing to give his word, but too superstitious to give his oath. He said that any way it was a Protestant Bible, and he would be sworn only on a Catholic Bible! Seeing that it was hopeless to get him to take his oath, I reluctantly accepted his word alone, and then told him nearly all the truth about myself. I now look upon it as almost an insane procedure. Fortunately, nothing ever resulted from my disclosures. Strangely, although it soon became known to all my associates of Mulberry Street that I was a college student and came from the best quarter of the city, no one ever attempted to follow me home or to blackmail me. These young men had never heard of this kind of blackmail.

After revealing who I was, I solemnly put the following questions, to all of which he answered in the affirmative, although never meaning to keep his word:

"Will you place me higher in your regard than any of your pals, seeing I am to you as a wife?

"Do you realize that you and I are united by a closer bond than that which unites you to your most intimate chums and pals?

"Will you then confide to me your secrets as to no one else in the world, and also share all my secrets?

"Will you regard our association as not merely for sensuous enjoyment, but also for close friendship, and for mutual help in the trials of life?"

Thus was cemented an androgyne's marriage bond. My purpose was to draw him away from his environment, and bring him up to my own social level, but my efforts met with complete failure.

Though having had in my career as a fairie about eight hundred intimates, I have had less than a score who formed an inner circle and whom I regarded as "husbands" *par excellence*. I only had one of them at a time, and our relations were long-continued. In the case of nearly every one of them, if it had been a matter dependent on my will, he would have been my life partner. But circumstances beyond my control brought a change on an average once a year. As a fairie, however, I was not satisfied with monandry. I sometimes applied the term "husband" playfully to my ordinary intimates.

These nights on Mulberry Street or vicinity had a great fascination for me, and in subsequent years continued to have a fascination. For a decade I occasionally yearned to be back there with the companions of these days of my fairie apprenticeship. With half a score of adolescents and two or three young women, an evening would be spent in some humble two-room apartment. Everybody was exceedingly happy, and I perhaps the happiest of all, sitting now in one young man's lap, and now in that of another. And how we all did sing! The young men petted and babied me more than they did any of the girls, and even right before the eyes of the girls. The latter were not jealous of me, especially because I was the one who financed these parties. In my actions I was far more feminine and babyish than any of the girls, and also far more amorous and skilled in coquetry. The girls thought nothing strange of me, as the nature of fairies was well known to them. I wish it understood, however, that these gatherings were no more indecent than a children's party in the best social stratum. Even these knights of Mulberry Street had their sense of decency. At these home parties, extreme intimacies were allowed only in private. The only refreshment was beer, the three-quart pail passing around the room from mouth to mouth, and being repeatedly sent out to be refilled. I alone did not partake, having, as already indicated, been brought up a total abstainer.

I have always been indifferent to the vast majority of men. I could sleep with them without becoming in the least excited. It was necessary to be under thirty, athletic, physically brave, smooth-shaven, and in no way deformed. On the other hand, throughout my open career of twelve years as a fairie, the proportion of men over thirty years old that sought intimacy was hardly more than one percent, while ninety-five percent were between eighteen and twenty-five.

During my apprenticeship just described, however, I was attracted only toward the ages sixteen to twenty-five, inclusive. Throughout this autobiography, I use the term "adolescent" to denote men within these age limits. Always has it seemed to me that men gradually grow less masculine and less virile (in coitus) after passing twenty-five. They have also appeared to me to lose their good looks soon after that age. To me man appears to grow old and his beauty fade a decade earlier than woman, which is just the opposite of the normal man's impression. When I was a boy of twelve, all males over sixteen appeared ugly, and I had only sexual disgust for them. But in 1918, when I have arrived at my middle forties, the age of male beauty in my eyes is confined between eighteen and thirty years.

I have always preferred the brunette to the blonde type, although I myself am of the former. For years after my fairie apprenticeship I seemed to be especially drawn toward young men of Irish blood. The pure Italian type of beauty, however, appears to me the highest. In my own veins flows blood of five different nationalities of western Europe, but no Irish or Italian. Perhaps my predilection for these two is due to the fact that they constituted exclusively my associates during my apprenticeship.

Large frame counted for a great deal, as also large and well-developed membra virilia. Variety exists as much in the latter respect as in respect to frame. There is often an inverse proportion between the two.

I much preferred the rough to the gentleman, and the profane boozing libertine to the morally upright. I have always been strongly attracted by disregard for personal danger. When reading accounts of exploration and adventure, I have sometimes fallen in love with the adventurer. For example, I fell in love with a noted Arctic explorer while reading his book, as well as with the kayakmen whose courageous deeds he describes. To me tattooing has always been the mark of supreme masculinity. It was a habit with me to seek for it on my beaux, and if found, I would rave over it, osculate it, kneel before the young blood in adoration, and call him all the glorious idealizing names I could think of. That one of my eight hundred beaux with whom I would have chosen to live out my life in daily comradeship was by far the most tattooed of all, and he did actually live with me for several months when I was forty years of age, besides being my "adopted son" for nine years. But it was not the tattooing alone that attracted me. In practically every manly charm, he stood supreme.

After an hour or so spent with a companion, it was painful to say good-by, and I generally hoped for another meeting. But subsequently to my apprenticeship just described, I generally had the same companion only once, or at most several times, as it was a long time, if ever, before we saw one another again. I usually felt for my companions a non-sensual wifely love in addition to the mere sexual attraction, which wifely love was transformed into a parental love after I had reached my middle thirties and my associates were ten or more years younger than myself. Throughout my life as a fairie, I always longed to have a young man live with me as my husband. If this had been practicable, monandry would possibly have been sufficient, as it proved to be in my early forties. But until long after the close of my open career, I was reluctant to reveal my identity, and was also deterred by the fear of blackmail.

At my middle forties, however, I am of the opinion that in the case of inverts, promiscuity is preferable to monandry for the welfare of the human race, the invert's associates individually, and the naturally polyandrous invert himself. Promiscuity does not affect the increase of the race, whereas monandry might by interfering with the young man's ultimately marrying a woman. Practically all the invert's intimates do this ultimately, and raise a family. It appears to be the natural function of the invert to minister to the ultra-virile until they reach marriageable age according to present-day standards. These relations merely supplant solitary onanism on the part of the virile, or else extra-marital relations with a young member of the gentle sex.

In my extensive experience, I have come across nothing to support the *a priori* view of some medical men that the adolescent tends to become a pervert, losing his normal instinct in whole or in part. My intimates of early childhood grew up to be fathers. None of my beaux of my apprenticeship just described—the only period of my adult career when I went repeatedly with the same ones—ever gave evidence of any growing coldness toward the gentle sex. Dozens of experiences that they individually had were without any such effect. Why should fellatio have such a tendency any more than occasional solitary onanism, to which practically all ultra-virile adolescents are subject? That this tendency is at most only a very remote possibility is indicated by the fact that the young man who was my "adopted son" for nine years was as much of a Don Juan at the end as at the beginning.

Secondly, invert promiscuity is to the interest of the young man because it would be cruel and unnatural to ask any one to remain permanently in the relation, and the promiscuity in question would obviate practically all risk of his ever becoming a pervert, if there be such risk.

Associates have told me that in coitus I was the most violently excited of any one they ever saw, and manifested the intensest feeling (*i.e.*, mental). A few have said that they preferred fellatio with me to the normal with a physical girl, while many have said whether the latter or a fairie was indifferent. Up to my early thirties, they always regarded me as a girl and used the feminine pronoun.

My original and fundamental method was active fellatio, the identical act of an infant ad matrem, quoad fuit emissio in comite, who would lie absolutely inactive. Time from a second to over an hour. Average time, about five minutes. In a very few, there was no result. If it had not been for the extreme weakening effect I would have been glad to lie inactive for an hour preceding and for another hour following, merely cum membro virili in ore. Generally cruria involvebant corpus meum, and I desired that premeret me cum iis aliquando. I would occasionally emit infantile vocables; for example, half-sobbing, or the natural language expressive of satisfaction and contentment. At other times I would express my admiration in a rather babyish manner: "Big, big, fierce fighter! Big, big desperado!" He would stroke my hair or face or pat me on the back, and say, "Poor baby!" "My cry-baby!" "Pet!" etc.

All other methods were taught me, for example, passive fellatio, which occurred at least as often as active because my companion preferred it, while I preferred the active. In the passive, I was completely so, and would often lie flat on my back. He would conduct himself the same as in normal coitus, often cum manibus conjunctis post caput meum, quoad habuit emissionem. During this action on the part of the majority, I suffered the greatest physical discomfort and saepe strangulatus sum. Dorsum oris has been often rendered sore, and the uvula was elongated, necessitating truncation because the elongation caused a chronic cough. I know of another invert who had to undergo the same operation. But I counted it happiness to suffer thus and endure pain when inflicted by a strong, brave, and rough young blood.

I say to readers who judge me to be horribly depraved for submitting to such usage: Nature created me puellam sine vagina, and then drew me toward the sturdy sex as few of the gentle sex are drawn. In such a case, what is more natural than to use the next best foramen? Furthermore, instinct pointed out the makeshift. It came just as natural for me utor ore as for physical women to use what Nature has provided them. In general, all through my life, whenever I have encountered virum who appeared to me as exceptionally beautiful, a strong desire has immediately arisen membrum virile in ore recipere. There are inverts guilty of such practices who in all other respects are exemplars of the highest morality. They even sometimes occupy the highest social station. They are blameless, and simply to be pitied.

Sometimes there was an alternation between the two methods, or both were adopted simultaneously. In the active, I did not have a fixed purpose inducendi ejaculationem in comite, neque desideravi semen. It was the mere act sugere that was my objective, and that gave me a sense of restful satisfaction. Nevertheless I practically semper devorabam. For days afterward it was a pleasure to reflect that what had once been the substance amatissimi was now my substance, and that the particles of matter that were once carried along in his veins, now floated in mine. In many cases I yearned to become the mother of his child, and often playfully spoke with an associate as if I had. Sometimes on meeting a young mother with her infant in her arms, I have wished to be in her place.

While lying cum membro virili in ore, I often feigned sleep, experiencing a sort of blissful dreaming, realizing that I was for a short season physically united to my mental and physical complement and opposite from whom fate and necessity separated me most of the time.

Even before castration, rarely expertus sum ejaculationem. During my fairie apprenticeship, however, it occurred about once in ten fellationes. But it was accompanied by such horrible feelings and thoughts that I used my will power to prevent it. This probably made it become less and less common during coitus, although from the age of sixteen until I was castrated at the age of twenty-eight, it averaged twice a week during sleep. When it occurred during coitus, I wanted everything to stop immediately, and felt like never again indulging therein. From the age of nineteen on, however, it was not quite so terrible as in my early teens. Paedicatio nunquam induxit ejaculationem in me, and under force, not even an orgasm.

Fellatio appears to be deeply rooted in the constitution of man and of the mammals in general, although usually coming to the surface only in exceptional individuals or under exceptional circumstances. It has been witnessed between dogs on the street and between monkeys in zoos. Guinea sows, when the boar is disinclined to coitus, repeatedly resort to a sort of fellatio, which appears to give the boar pleasure. Fellatio is common in the underworld between the two sexes. In a 1915 issue of the *Alienist and Neurologist*, a writer maintained that fellatio is common among ordinary respectable married pairs.

My peculiar instinct was the occasion recipiendi in stomachum in tantum novem portiones liquoris vitae in one evening. There was never any tonic or other beneficial effect. The apparent effect is an immediate disagreeable stimulation, followed the next day by a serious mental and physical collapse. This depression was, however, not specially serious during my first two or three years of promiscuity. Possibly later my constitution had become somewhat undermined and coitus therefore became more fatiguing. The collapse was particularly severe after I was castrated at the age of twenty-eight. Cultured inverts of strong passions realize the detriment to their health from coitus, yet they feel that it is the *summum bonum* for which everything else should be sacrificed. My own fascination for the rough and wild-natured was so great that for a decade I could not let slip a single opportunity.

Sometimes for several days following fellatio, I would suffer from a slight fever and all my organs and muscles would seem to be used up, as if I was just about to expire from exhaustion. I would be very irritable, and nothing seemed to go as it should. My brain was particularly affected, and during the latter half of my open career as a fairie, I would be incapable of doing good mental work for two or three days following an indulgence. My judgment and critical faculties were clouded, and I could do only such work as was mechanical in its nature. Providence endowed me with powers of mind such as are met with in approximately one alone out of two score university graduates. In life I have achieved about the average success of a university graduate. I have every reason to believe that if it had not been for my suffering for twelve years from acute spermatorrhea, and if I had been able to abstain wholly from coitus, I would have reached the front rank among university men. I therefore exhort young intellectual inverts to be continent as far as possible. For every indulgence, a heavy penalty must be paid in diminished efficiency. For each minute of bodily contact with a counterpart that I have enjoyed, I have had to pay one hour of resultant serious suffering, physical or mental.

My mind and body have, however, always been hypersensitive to all stimuli and impressions. A few swallows of tea or coffee after one P.M. would make me lie awake half the night. A slightly tainted article of food which would have no effect on most people would prostrate me mentally and physically for hours afterward. A business worry would cause me to lie awake for hours. When spending the night in bed with one to whom I was attracted, I generally lay awake the whole night, and for this reason, I usually sought a separate place to sleep in.

But all these bad effects following fellatio I have sometimes fancied might be due rather to the mere presence of membri virilis in ore and in juxtaposition to the brain. The debilitating effects of coitus inter femora or of paedicatio were not one-quarter as marked as those of fellatio. Moreover, perhaps the ill effects of departures from the entirely normal form of coitus are roughly proportional to the extent of departure. Fellatio is further removed from normal coitus than inter femora or paedicatio. On a few occasions, as an experiment, exspui semen, but it seemed to make no difference in the aftereffects. Quite probably the bad effects were due to a relapse after intense nervous excitement, which in my case always accompanied fellatio, but not paedicatio, which latter I never sought. Or it might have been largely due to my habitual inhibition of the ejaculatory center. I now believe that I made a mistake in respect to this inhibition, and that it is more healthful to experience the exclamation than to check it by force of will.

Not until I reached the age of thirty-nine did I, by chance, discover a means to alleviate decidedly the exhausting effects of fellatio. I had used potassium iodide extensively in tablet form dissolved in water for syphilis. I discovered it to be for me an excellent sedative and soporific, and occasionally used it to secure this effect alone. I further discovered that fifteen to twenty grains taken at night after fellatio almost entirely forestalled the exhaustion otherwise supervening on the following days. Experience further taught me at about the age of thirty-nine that the supervening exhaustion was in large measure forestalled by eating a light lunch several minutes before fellatio, and a hearty meal as soon afterwards as possible. Fellatio occurring just before rising in the morning was found to induce far less fatigue than when occurring in the evening, or at night just before going to sleep.

On rare occasions—about one hundred out of sixteen hundred—we adopted the normal position, cum peni ejus inter femora mea. I was entirely passive. It was necessary for me ponere femur unum transversum altero in order to form a foramen strictum. Sometimes I requested this pose, and sometimes my companion. This was the nearest to normal coitus. I was curious to see how my companion would conduct himself with a genuine fille.

Only when I could not avoid it, either because of force or because of insistent entreaty on the part of a kind companion, paedicatio took place. I would sometimes be beaten into submission, and knives would be drawn on me by the most desperate ruffians of the slums. Anus evidenter attrahit a very small percentage of men, just as the pudenda does the normal individual. Tangebant atque dicebant, "Anus pulcher." My intense moral horror of paedicatio experienced at the beginning of my fairie days gradually declined. I later enjoyed it somewhat only because I enjoyed witnessing all kinds of amorous conduct on the part of ultra-virile young men. I had a craze to see them sexually excited, and to see the means they instinctively took to appease their ardor. The pain to me was generally excruciating—ad magnitudinem priapi—and has sometimes rendered walking painful for months together. It also occasionally brought on hemorrhoids of brief duration, but so painful as to render walking almost impossible. It is attended with much risk to the pathic. I know of two who were compelled to undergo serious operations as a result of repeatedly permitting it, one of whom in his early forties was invalided for the rest of his life. In my own case, paedicatio occurred only about fifty times out of sixteen hundred instances of coitus.

Up to the age of thirty, two years after castration, I was seemingly never satisfied. I have expressed to a group of companions the wish to die through them as did the Levite's concubine at Gibeah, as related in the Book of Judges. In the subsequent physical and mental collapse, I received comfort from the consciousness that it was the result of devotion to adored beings.

When spasmus in my companion was impossible otherwise, I would resort to manustupration. My companions preferred me to do this rather than do it themselves. Only twice in all my career did my companion do it to me, much against my wishes. I have always had a horror of this experience, including solitary onanism.

Except for these two instances, and one instance when a companion to my disgust attempted fellatio, my pudenda never had any part in coitus, and I always wished I was rid of them. No method ever brought me any kind of local physical pleasure. That is, I am entirely devoid of any erogenous center. Companions have remarked that sensus gratissimus suffunderet corpus totum. I never experienced anything of the kind in the least degree. With me the satisfaction was practically all mental. I found it exclusively in the body of my associate, not at all in my own. I was satisfied with the realization that I was instrumental in efficiendo ei voluptatem acutam. I had my pleasure in seeing his vita sexualis strongly aroused and in witnessing the manifestations of the procreative instinct in him, e.g., his me cogendum, detrahendum mihi vestem, ejus appetitionem propellendi, anhelandum, etc. I was happy in the thought that I was being received tanquam uxorem by a handsome high-spirited adolescent. He called me uxorem, and I called him maritum. There was also a life-long satisfaction in the remembrance that I had possessed him in amplexu sexuali. To mimic the baby and the woman in his presence was a rare pleasure. Up to my early thirties, in all my conduct with him, I was more feminine than any woman and as babyish as a three-year old. Sexually I have never grown out of babyhood.

I liked to be regarded as the slave. In the "Enslaving Ceremony," I lay prostrate on the floor, my companion towered above, placed his foot on my head, and pronounced me his slave. I have always felt that a woman should adore her husband so much as to delight in being treated as a slave, and to suffer gladly any abuse by her lord.

In the "Ceremony of Adoration," my companion stood upright, I prostrated myself, clasped his legs, pressed my lips against his feet, recited all the heroic qualities which enslaved me to him, and cried out over and over again my love and adoration for him. Associates have said they only hoped they would ultimately secure a wife who would adore them as I.

I sometimes found pleasure in my companion being vexed with me and striking me. I would playfully slap him until he was provoked to give me a blow meant seriously. With heartless associates who were bent merely on the pleasure spasmi and would choke and otherwise maltreat me into submission to paedicatio, I often enjoyed being thus forced. Occasionally I even insisted that friendly ones rapere for the pleasure of struggling to get away and feeling their conquering strength.

There was a great difference in respect to the extent to which they responded. Some would not allow osculation above the waist and only desired spasmum. From this coldness there were all grades up to the associates who would kiss and hug me, and even let me protrudere linguam in os ejus, atque vice versa.

Although a girl only in mind, though to some extent in body, this deficiency seemed not to detract from my success in the vocation of a fille de joie. Few filles have had a clientele the equal of mine in youthfulness, beauty, and virility. Providence compensated me for my years of grief over being an invert by throwing in my way this exceptional clientele. My enterprise in seeking conquests was that usually found in the male, and rarely in the female.

Practically all my companions have remained permanently a part of me. Now and then through life when the memory of a particular one arises, it has been accompanied by regret at the thought of our eternal separation, and by the consciousness that I was offering him an eternal worship of which he could never know. From my late twenties on, I impressed it upon my ever changing companions that I offered them an eternal worship, and that down through life, when we must be forever separated, they should think of me as still offering them my adoration.

I am now going to recount how I happened to abandon Mulberry Street as my "stamping ground" when I had so many accommodating friends there. On account of a nervous breakdown, due partly to overstudy, partly to debauchery, but chiefly to emissions during sleep which had afflicted me twice a week since the age of sixteen, I was unable to stay out my junior year in college and left the city the middle of May. I was to spend my last evening with my "husband" *par excellence* at a theatre. I was to meet him at seven o'clock on a Broadway corner several blocks from his usual haunts. Since I did not expect to be with him where he could help himself to my belongings, and also since I had to leave my residence before dark, instead of putting on cast-off clothing as usual on my visits to the foreign-born quarters, I clad myself in my best and wore a gold ring and watch and chain.

But he did not come, though I waited a half-hour in anguish. It was only five minutes' walk from his usual haunts, but clad as I was, I was afraid to seek him there. Finally two Italian bootblacks happened to pass. Even the boys of that part of Mulberry Street knew me. I however never had anything to do with them, not being attracted toward those immature sexually. Even my companions would always drive away boys who sought to stand around our group. The bootblacks now called out: "Hello Jennie! Where yer goin' all dressed up?"

I sent a message by them, and waited still another half-hour. Of all things in the world, I wanted at that moment a sight of my idol. Though realizing the risk I was running, I decided that I must go nearer to his usual haunts. I walked to the corner of Mulberry. I said to myself that I would not venture any farther. I would wait on this corner until he happened to pass, since it was on his route home. I considered myself safe since the street was well lighted and there were numerous pedestrians.

After waiting here also a half-hour in vain, I became hysterical, wept, wrung my hands, and gave utterance to suppressed shrieks. I finally decided the only thing to do was to walk up Mulberry Street. About the middle of the block, I happened to find him seated, as usual, in a group of my beaux. They all made exclamations of surprise and pleasure when they caught sight of me. It was my first and only appearance there dressed up. My mate called out: "Hello pretty little girl!"

"Hello big, brave, bouncing boy!"

They immediately pulled me down to a seat among them and several hands were stuck into my pockets. I had tucked my bills away in the waistband of my trousers. The street was alive with recent Italian immigrants, and I might have saved my coin by raising an alarm, but of course did not choose to. On every visit here I had my pockets rifled, and did not mind the loss of the coin.

My mate sought to be as captivating as possible, and put me in a state of perfect happiness. Before long he asked me to sleep with him and a pal that night. All this time, among this group of young bloods, there was but one female, only sixteen years of age, whose home was on this block. It was decided that we should spend the night in her rooms. Accompanied by the two ruffians and the young woman, I thus finally sauntered down a pitch-dark alley and descended some steps to the basement of a ramshackle rear tenement, occupied entirely by illiterate Italians recently immigrated. I revolted at what I saw and smelt, but on this and other occasions was drawn by sexual attraction into pestilential places where nothing else would have induced me to remain a minute.

When the lamp was lighted, I found myself in a suite of two dilapidated rooms, scantily and poorly furnished. On a century-old bedstead rested a dirty mattress filled with straw, and no pillows or bed-linen. Benefiting by my money, my associates drank to excess as the evening wore away, while I found my pleasure in the usual manner. Toward midnight, after the two ruffians had become half-intoxicated, my mate placed the muzzle of a revolver, which the young woman kept for self-defence, against my head, saying he would blow my brains out if I got him into any trouble. Because of the maudlin condition of the two young men, and because I had something on me that they might consider worth committing a grave crime for, I now half expected never to leave the place alive, and repeatedly breathed a prayer that no serious harm might be permitted to befall me. I now let them dispossess me of the balance of my bills and my other valuables in dismay and without the slightest protest, for fear of angering them.

Finally, in order to frighten me further from making complaint to the police, one of the ruffians asked the other whether they should put a bullet through my head or turn me over to the police because of my peculiar addiction. Thoroughly frightened, I implored them to let me go home. After some deliberation, designed to show how they had me in their power, including the assurance that I had that night rendered myself liable to a long term of imprisonment—ignorant men always thinking only the androgyne is amenable to the law—they finally decided to let me go if I ran away from the neighborhood as fast as my legs would carry me. The three of them escorted me to the mouth of the alley, and the last words I caught were: "Run faster! Run faster!"

While in college I shrunk from the required gymnasium exercises. I felt that they were proper for young men, but my feminine nature made me exceedingly shy while in line in the drill. In the gymnasium dressing-room I would enjoy seeing the naked forms, but concealed my own. If military drill had been required, as is the case in some universities in 1918, it would have caused me to omit a university education.

Beginning about this time, my twenty-first year, and continuing down to the date when this book goes to press, I have commonly worn in my home an ornamental bathrobe, just like a woman's dress. Clad in it, I have gazed at my reflection in the mirror, imagining I was a woman. Walking in it to and fro and up and down the stairs, I have taken pleasure in hearing it rustle like a woman's dress, in feeling it strike against my legs, and in holding it up when ascending the stairs, as a woman her skirts. In my college days, while home for week-ends, I would occasionally, when alone, put on a sister's hat and gaze at myself in the mirror with rare pleasure, wishing that I might wear that style of hat.

In this summer of 1894, when away from New York, where temptation was less strong, I became for several weeks weaned away from my peculiar habits. In my present rather puritanical circle, I felt like a wolf in sheep's clothing. Under the unusual religious influences, I even thought I might never again seek the gratification of my peculiar cravings.

Nevertheless, before many weeks, I began to suffer intensely from sexual starvation and melancholia. Being then a nervous wreck, I saw before me only insanity or suicide. I would walk deserted streets at night beating my breast and waving my arms in anguish. Even in broad daylight and on the main street, I several times wept openly while walking along, so that people who knew me probably thought I was insane. In the privacy of my room I would writhe on my bed in an agony of tears.

My sexual cravings began to render me sleepless after retiring, and throw me into paroxysms. Driven by my importunate craving for fellatio, I would occasionally rise from bed around midnight, and roam through the poor quarters, looking for a thoroughly intoxicated man who would not be able to recognize me, but I never found one. I now believe I was irresponsible.

The only ray of hope I had was the possibility of securing a steady mate. When in my imagination I could see the feasibility and certainty of this, I was happy and hopeful. I felt that then a successful life would be a certainty. Without a mate I feared for my virtue and my reputation. With one I felt that I could live a virtuous life outside of occasional fellatio with him. At the present time (1918), I am convinced that I had a right view of the matter back there in 1894. Possession of a mate would have been the panacea for all my ills.

My New York physician, to whom I confided my woes, wrote that the only remedy to make me well and happy was the possession of a mate, and urged me to apply immediately to some stalwart acquaintance. I decided to appeal to a cousin, an adolescent fair to look upon, and possessed of all the qualities of mind attractive to the female sex. Moreover, in my early childhood, he had been one of my intimates. Too much ashamed to speak, I handed him the following argument:

". . . I am driven to make these disclosures to you, or else go insane or commit suicide. I am madly in love with you. I say it before God— this impulse of my being is entirely opposed to my will. I bewail the fact that this animality is a part of my nature. I abhor sensual love and sensual enjoyment, and if I had my choice, would never stoop to them. Nevertheless, sometimes a person cannot do what he would but what he must. My physician says my health demands that I do not resist this overpowering impulse. Last night I went to bed drowsy and tired. But the impossibility of my possessing the masculine counterpart which nature ordained I should have, threw me for an hour into paroxysms which threatened to take away all my strength. I had finally to leave my bed, and spend two hours reading in order to save myself from insane raving. The statement of the few specialists who have studied into the nature of sexual inversion is that the craving of a person like myself for his sexual counterpart is abnormally intense, and that it is, for the ends of health, more necessary for his peculiar craving to be met than it is necessary for the normal man or woman's.

"Judging from the past, my life is likely to be a wreck if I deny this instinctive craving. In leading a life of chastity, I have endured a melancholy existence, and have often deliberated suicide. Recently I have meditated it daily. All my privileges, which one would think must make my life a happy one, have failed to make life to me worth living. You may say it is my own fault, and that I just make my own life miserable. But truly, it is a matter to me not dependent on my will power, but on physiological and psychological laws, over which the will has no more control than over the diphtheria.

"That I desire such indulgence does not spring from the fact that I have become licentious or a debauchee, placing my own selfish sensual enjoyment above everything else. I am as ardent as ever in my yearnings to alleviate human misery and to deny myself for others. But in this matter, the result of my denying myself would be almost as serious as to resolve to give up eating for the sake of saving the money for the cause of missions. There are some things which it would be fatal to us to give up, even if we did it through motives of altruism. I assure you that I have not abandoned my high aspirations and worthy aims of life.

"I assert before God that I am confident that I commit no sin in obeying this instinct. During my moments of closest communion with God, I am sensible of His smile on my conduct in this matter. In general the only legitimate relations are between a legally married pair. The marriage state is open to the normal man and he is duty bound to marry when passion becomes too strong. This duty however is not binding on urnings,[2] because they cannot get any one to marry them. I endeavored to marry a young man in New York, but failed. Therefore it is in consonance with the moral law for urnings to enjoy the company of those they love without marrying.

"You may reply that such relations are prohibited in the Bible. Relations between man and man, both of whom are normal, are prohibited. But in the past year I have learned that I am seven-eighths a woman, and only one-eighth man.[*] Were it not for certain masculine conformations of the body, I ought to go about in dresses as a woman, and always identify myself with the female sex. Therefore, I being more a woman than a man, these prohibitions in the Bible do not apply to me.

"I think I have satisfied you that I can without sin follow out my desire in the way Nature prompts. But I would convince you that my companion also acquiesces in my desire without sin. I would not wish to allure any one into obliging me unless he could see that he was thereby committing no sin. There is sin only in those things which rob God of His glory, or which bring unhappiness and detriment to some sentient being. In this case, if sin at all, it would be sin against self. But by it you harm yourself in no way, as the physician told me.

---

2. At that time I incorrectly described myself as an urning. Urnings are, at least usually, active pederasts, or else addicted to mutual onanism.

* This early statement may be too strong. Psychically I am practically all woman, and physically at least one-third, although the organs of generation are completely male.

"Then too, urnings, congenital as I, are the work of God, the divine purpose in their creation being probably to check a too rapid increase in the population; and God must therefore have meant that their instinctive cravings for a sexual counterpart should be gratified, especially since he has made these cravings doubly intense. But how could they be gratified without the acquiescence of some normal individual? Therefore the latter is also without sin.

"I am not now, as you may think, writing in a state of extreme excitement, such as I might be in in the presence of the attractive person, when I would not be my true self; but I am writing in a comparatively calm, rational frame of mind. I am backed up in what I write by an experienced physician, whose letter I can show you, and who says that if I had the occasional satisfaction of this craving, I would become healthy, get rid of my morbid thoughts, and have some vim for work, and for distinguishing myself as a scholar. I am myself confident that with this occasional gratification I would some day win the admiration of the circles of religion and learning for my scholarly attainments and for my work for humanity.

"All I ask is that you take a common-sense, rational view of the matter. If there is still any doubt in your mind about your possible compliance being compatible with honor and morality, please state your difficulty, and I assure you I can remove it, since I have given much study to the ethics of this question. . ."

BUT HE ABSOLUTELY DECLINED TO grant the favor asked, giving as his only reason that it would be "self-pollution." In culture, education, and broadness of mind, he stood much below me, but he had some religious scruples, and also his tastes were naturally against compliance. I made further oral solicitations, but he remained deaf to them. I was plunged into despair at his refusal to listen to reason, and my head was drooping in shame. With an intense impulse for self-destruction possessing me, I turned my steps toward a stream about a mile away, where I intended to blot out my miserable existence. But when I had walked some distance, the beauties of nature gradually drew away my thoughts from my chagrin.

Since this cousin was my only hope during the many weeks that I had still to remain in the village, and since I was madly attracted to him, I did not give up all endeavor. Later happenings are described in the following letter to my New York physician:

". . . I write to you in order to see if I can be saved from insanity. Last night I again appealed to my cousin, with whom I am deeply in love. I called at his house about nine o'clock, but he was not in. I told his mother I would go up to his room and wait for him. Finally he appeared. I was simply going to ask him to let me kiss him. If he had granted only this, I would have gone home happy and contented. He could not see me, as the room was in darkness, but as soon as he heard me, he said he would shoot me if I did not clear out immediately, and he made a move to get his revolver, which he always keeps loaded under his pillow. I entreated him not to shoot, and to let me say merely a few words; but he answered angrily, 'If you do not leave the house immediately, I will put a bullet through your head!'

"I immediately left quite calmly, but after I got in my own bed, I began to cry over my cousin's treatment of me. All of a sudden, without any conscious volition, I sat up in bed, threw my legs and arms about wildly, and for a few seconds shrieked loudly and frightfully. This paroxysm has left me in a state of complete exhaustion, and I now do not know whether I am sane or insane.

"No one can sympathize with me. My cousin, an honorable and intelligent young man, now knows much about my case, and how I have suffered for years, and yet I received from him last night only harsh words, emphasized by a revolver. Such treatment by one I dearly love drives me crazy. If only he had denied my request in gentle words, I would have gone home and merely wept tears of gratitude at his forbearance. . ."

I longed to be back in a great city, where alone life is possible for such as me provided one wishes to preserve a good reputation. But I did not have the means to go, nor anything I could give my parents as a pretext. After the last terrible repulse, I left my cousin alone. But I was still frequently driven late at night to wander about the village, hoping to find some man in a thoroughly intoxicated condition, but many, many weary hours were thus spent in a vain search.

I now learned that a detachment of light artillery, stationed at a fort near New York City, who were out on a practice march, would camp in a neighboring town. This news enchanted me, and I informed my parents that I was going off for a trip afoot for a few days, of course not making known my motive. Though a nervous wreck, I was at the time able to walk twenty miles a day.

I reached the camp toward sunset. With other civilians, I lingered around until late in the evening. I tried to enter into conversation with the young soldiers, who fascinated me, but could not overcome my bashfulness. Finally, after most of them had retired, I left the camp, and started off to seek lodging for the night. But on the way I unexpectedly met a tall soldier of imposing appearance, and by a great effort of the will, I stepped up, walked along by his side, and entered into conversation.

When from his words and manner I judged that he was kindhearted and would not take advantage of my own unfortunate position in society, I threw off the role of a male, and gave full swing to the feminine side of my nature. My long enforced abstinence had driven me wild, and I now poured out hot protestations of love and adoration. Finding that they were received sympathetically, I threw myself into his arms, clasped my hands around his neck, and wept for happiness. The effect on me of the soldier's charms was beyond description. His face and head seemed to be surrounded with a halo of glory. There was an air about him so careless, so sensual, so brave, so manly, and yet so kind. I called him by all the names which love can invent in order to deify its object. He however soon had to retire to the camp, and left me heartsick.

I again started toward town, and soon met another soldier, who happened to be in a maudlin condition. Because of this, I thought I had nothing to fear, and accosted him in such a way as to disclose my nature immediately without first sounding to see if he was of a compassionate nature. Though not at all offended, but laughing at what he considered an amusing experience, and expressing his willingness, he demanded five dollars, and said that unless I handed it over, he would take me before the captain of his company. This was said merely to frighten me, but in my greenness, I fully believed he would do it. Thoroughly alarmed, I started off on a run. The soldier staggered after, crying, "Catch him! Catch him!" In a moment there were three other soldiers and a constable in pursuit. I was caught, the constable took me in hand, and asked what it was all about. Before any one else could reply, I addressed the five supplicatingly:

"I am ashamed to tell it, but I am an urning.* I simply asked this soldier to do me a favor, to which he certainly did not object, because he only laughed. I have not done anything to him wrong or criminal. I only proposed something, and then he said he would take me before his captain unless I paid him five dollars. I became frightened and ran away. I pray you, have mercy on me, and let me go. If you knew what a sad life I have had, you would feel sorry for me. I have felt like committing suicide a thousand times. I am not willingly what I am. It is my misfortune and not my fault that I am an urning. If you are ever capable of compassion, let my fate move you to pity. Please let me go and don't arrest me!"

The soldiers soon went on their way, and the constable conducted me in the direction of the lockup. He acted toward me as if I was a low criminal, while I continued to supplicate him to let me go. As we came nearer the lockup, in my highly excited condition over the fear of disgracing my family, who lived only four miles away, and the prospect that if my secret was disclosed, I could never see any of my loved ones again, I thoughtlessly declared I would not go any farther, which caused him to rap my head with his club.

I was locked up for the night. Through nervous shock, I did not sleep a wink. Only to the few is it given ever to taste such a night of misery as I passed. "I, whom all think the purest and most pious of men, being arrested!" I meditated. "I, the last one whom anybody would have expected ever to be arrested! But God's will be done. . . Am I to be the one to disgrace my family? Hitherto I have been the scholar, the litterateur, the only collegian of my father's family, and have by my achievements in learning brought the most honor on my father's house of all his children. I shall also be the one to bring the deepest disgrace upon it."

The following morning I was sentenced to three days in the lock-up. As the village of my incarceration was only four miles from my home, and I was known at least by sight to some of its inhabitants, my father evidently soon learned of my disgrace, notwithstanding that I had sought to conceal my identity. Although he never mentioned the episode, he soon began to treat me regularly with extreme bitterness, as if he wished I had never been born. I was the only one of his children to whom he manifested any such spirit, notwithstanding I was the brightest of them.

---

* Term misapplied.

EARL LIND

Throughout an entire decade subsequent to this episode, I had an unreasonable nervousness about arrest and about policemen. Whenever any one whose name was unfamiliar was announced as waiting to see me, my first thought and fear were that a policeman had come to arrest me. Whenever any one called me up on the telephone, I always feared that it was in connection with my forthcoming arrest.

A few days after being restored to liberty, I informed my parents of my intention to go off on another trip afoot, this time for a couple of weeks. My secret object was to mingle with this detachment of troops, whom I knew to be encamped for some weeks about two days' easy journey on foot from my home. That just described was my first experience with soldiers, and I had become fascinated as never before. All my reveries were now to relinquish the career of a scholar and become a sutler near some fort in the wild west so that I could mingle daily with these demigods, whom I most abjectly worshipped. I was in misery because my lot in life separated me from these ferocious young men.

I look upon a youthful professional soldier as a most wonderful being, different from all other human beings. There seems to be a sort of enchantment about him. Merely the process of enlistment, the donning of the uniform, and the acquiring of skill in handling the weapons of warfare make a demigod out of the young man, as your author looks upon it. When a newspaper item states that a trainload of *regular* soldiers passed through a certain town, I reflect with a thrill on what a wonderful burden that train bore, and experience a sense of pain that I could not be along and make known the adoration I feel. Ever since this my first encounter with regular soldiers, I have wished for omnipresence with the men of the regular army. Privates, corporals, and sergeants are men after my own heart. I was never attracted toward commissioned officers, and they have appeared to me as being less manly than the classes named. Perhaps my predilection is due to the fact that the commissioned officers are as a rule intellectual like myself. Subsequently to my reaching the age of twenty-five, regular soldiers have been practically the only young men to whom I have been strongly attracted. After that age I found it easy to relinquish coquetry with all other young men. Now (1918) when I have arrived at my middle forties, I pine alone not to be able longer—on account of my age—to mingle with regular soldiers as a mignon. As Ophelia with Othello, I love them and adore them for the dangers they have passed through, as well as those attached to their vocation. Furthermore, in man's natural state, fighting—next to procreating—is the pre-eminent function of the male. For this reason the war-loving man is my sexual ideal.

Arrived a short distance from the camp, I, for only the second time in my life, caught the thrilling notes of the bugle-call. It took all the strength out of my legs so that I felt as if I would fall to the ground. Since I began to associate with soldiers, the notes of the bugle have had an unearthly—I might say, an eternal, overwhelming—beauty. Subsequently to 1905, when my open career as a soldiers' mignon became a thing of the past, the bugle-call has made me live that career over again in a few moments. It brings up fond memories of the many evenings spent in the long, long ago with the "mighty men of war." It fills my soul with adoration for these "mighty men of valor," these "mighty men of renown." I have sometimes been seized with a babyish cooing or gasping, and have ardently wished that I were youthful again and in the arms of one of these wonderful beings.

The effect on me of secular music in general has been to arouse reveries of my amours and paramours. I have been an unusual lover and patron of grand opera, the soprano and alto solos having an overwhelming effect particularly (because that is the manner in which I would have wished to sing). I have often been raised into sublime heights of ecstasy, generally with a sensual tinge.

Arrived at the camp, I strolled about and was soon recognized: "Hello Pretty! Where did you come from?" Filled with bliss, and thrown into my most babyish and effeminate mood, I responded: "You adorable artilleryman, I was pining for you, and followed you here from X——." He told me to meet him outside the camp after retreat, when he appeared with several comrades. I was in ecstasy on this first walk of my life on a country road with a party of bewitching adolescent soldiers as daylight was fast fading into darkness. In my years of subsequent association with soldiers, I found that those over twenty-five years of age were in general disinclined to talk with me. They appeared to have been already satiated with flirtation, while numerous youngsters were desirous of a frolic with me.

Havelock Ellis says: "The homosexual tendency appears to have flourished chiefly among warriors and warlike peoples." In another place he says: "I have been told by medical men in India that it is specially common among the Sikhs, the finest soldier-race in India." I have myself found adolescent professional soldiers the easiest of conquests and the most inclined of any class of men to take the virile part with me. I speak from experience in flirtation with at least two thousand different professional soldiers, only about four hundred of whom, however, went to extremes. I saw not the least tendency toward homosexuality amongst themselves, although I frequented to some extent their barracks and even their bunks. They are only capable of taking the virile part with an individual like your author. In general the common soldiers of the regular army are particularly rough, coarse-grained, vigorous, and sensual men, constituting physically the best blood of the race. As already indicated, practically all civilians who were intimate with me were of this same type, and there appears to be some connection between tremendous virility and active homosexuality. Furthermore, along with this ultra-virility of the professional common soldier, he is almost entirely shut off from the gentle sex, whereas the young civilian of the laboring classes has usually an acquaintance who gladly yields as his mistress. Of course many of the nation's fighters have a natural distaste. As just indicated, only about one in five with whom I coquetted went to extremes, while about fifty percent of those who knew me by sight would never even speak to me. But the line of cleavage did not at all correspond with that between the religious or conscientious and the vicious. It was a matter as much outside the province of ethics as is vegetarianism.

Moreover, soldiers lead comparatively idle lives, and also monotonous lives, and these two conditions add to their susceptibility to the wiles of a fairie. A bright and facile fairie is capable of furnishing them a great deal of entertainment, aside from the opportunity of exercising their fundamental impulse. With myself also, *coitus was a comparatively small element* in our mutual relations. Innocent coquetry, including "taking off" the baby and the woman, occupied a far larger place.

My relations with a coterie of beaux, and particularly with soldiers around the camps and forts, reminded me sometimes a play. I was, as it were, acting a part. Perhaps it would be nearer the truth to say that another personality was in possession of me. I was conscious that I was the same "I" who was one of the leaders in scholarship at the university and who was there looked upon as a particularly innocent and pure-minded youth. I was also conscious that in the society of my beaux I was not acting as became the sensible, rational, respectable collegian of other occasions. I felt that I had temporarily relinquished my mind and body to the dictates of another spirit, that of a "baby-girl"—a combination of baby and girl. It was however a spirit not alien to me. It was a spirit which had dwelt in my brain from infancy. It was a spirit that had always been called up by the sight of beautiful stalwart males of the proper age. For the work of life I realized that this spirit would not do. If I was to make a name for myself in the world, I must dethrone this baby-spirit in me. When in my study, I sought to forget this baby-spirit. I even turned against it at times with a sort of abhorrence, and asked myself how I could give way to it. Thus I lived a sort of a two-sided life. Part of the time I was a sober-minded intellectual worker. Part of the time, when under sexual excitement, even to a slight degree, I displayed the mental traits of a baby. I knew that these two states, babyhood and adult manhood, were incongruous, but to have a contented mind and to be in a mood which would render a career devoted to scholarly pursuits possible, it was necessary occasionally to follow out my feminine and babyish instincts. It should be remembered, however, that I have never developed into a full-fledged man either physically or mentally. If my business associates tell the truth, I am still in 1918 a child nearly half a century old. Childlikeness is a common characteristic of androgynes.

I was not alone in acting a part when with a coterie of beaux, but they also did in conducting themselves toward me as if I were a girl. While strolling with soldiers through the fields and woods, I would demand assistance over places of the slightest difficulty, and some of them were marvellously solicitous under the circumstances. They instinctively yearned to be the protector of some weak female, and being deprived of practically all female company, they spent their instinctive gallantry on me. This was to me a rare pleasure.

In our drama, it was bliss to me to be the star, the center of attraction, the only representative of the gentle sex present, while there might be around me half a score of large, powerful young bloods. In my every-day sphere, I have been exceedingly shy, but as "Jennie June" I have impersonated a baby-girl before a hundred soldiers at a time without being in the least embarrassed. I would fret after the manner of a baby and sob just for the pleasure of having them soothe and pet me. I would pretend to faint away just for the pleasure of being caught in their arms and held there. When in the country, I sometimes feigned unwillingness to go with them, and forced them to carry me, with hands, arms, and whole body hanging limp. This was also a rare pleasure. Sometimes they would scare me in fun in order to bring from me a shrill feminine shriek—when I felt sure no officers or civilians were near. Indeed while in their company, I exaggerated cowardice, babyishness, and femininity in general.

On this visit of 1894 with the soldiers, most of them treated me well. Some even allowed me to call in their tents, and shared their meals with me. But others, who had been brought up to believe that a fairie must be a monster of wickedness, and were disinclined to learn through association with me that I was a paragon of morality apart from coquetry and venery, were bitterly opposed to my presence in the camp and sought to injure me. But I was treated so well by so many that I made myself too free. I was of course guilty of no immodesty or ultra-babyishness within the boundaries of the camp.

The increasing opposition culminated one afternoon. I had asked an acquaintance if I could take a nap in his bunk, and as a joke, he installed me in the bunk of an enemy. As a result I was ordered off the camp-ground. I had to traverse a lane lined with tents, in front of which their occupants were eating supper. As I passed, with head bowed in humiliation, the majority were laughing at me, while the malevolent called out the appropriate vulgar epithet, and threw scraps of food and cups of coffee into my face. I was wishing the earth might open and swallow me up. This experience led me to leave for home immediately.

As only a few weeks now remained before my return to New York to begin my senior year, I passed them without being tormented by unsatisfied instincts. On my return, I had no intention to seek my Mulberry Street friends, partly because of the events at our leave-taking in May, and partly because of the cooling of my fascination after four months' separation. I decided not to frequent the outlying fort where my soldier friends had returned because of the inconvenience of going thither. I believed I could find associates within a half-hour's journey from where I myself resided. I had decided to try my luck in the 14th Street theatre district, which was at that time a favorite promenade of fairies.

One evening I clad myself so as to present the most attractive appearance possible: a blue suit, with boxplaited, belted coat (Norfolk style); dark red necktie; white gloves; and patent-leather shoes. As a high-class fairie, I sought to dress in a distinctive manner, so as to be more readily recognized by my prey. Therefore unusually large neck bows and white gloves. Fairies are inclined to be loud in their dress. The excessive wearing of gloves and the wearing of a red neck-tie are almost universal with high-class fairies. Once a blackmailer to whom I would not hand out the three dollars demanded made good his threat to turn me over to a policeman, who took my red tie as conclusive evidence that

I was a fairie. Of a fairie who was arrested for accosting on the street, I have heard it said: "He got thirty days for wearing a red tie."

On my first visit to the theatre district named, I promenaded up and down for about an hour, afraid to accost any adolescent. Finally one accosted me: "How's business?"

"How do you know my business?" I replied with a smile.

"Oh, I know all right. Didn't you get many tonight?"

"I was only looking for you. I cannot express how beautiful you appear to me. Please excuse me for being so outspoken."

"Oh, there's no harm done."

"You are the most beautiful and best dressed fellow I have seen this evening. Won't you please, *please*, take me as your valet and slave? I will serve you for nothing."

He happened to be living in a furnished-room house in the neighborhood. Arrived in his room, he treated me with marvellous gallantry, as if I had been a queen. For several weeks, I spent an evening in his company. He introduced me to his companions, they to theirs in turn, and before long I numbered among my acquaintances scores of the habitues of the gambling halls and other dens of vice of this quarter of the city, and associated with them in these places, though fellatio and coquetry were my own only departures from a most puritanical life. Such an environment was it that fate had in store for the innocent stripling of a few years ago who had chosen for himself the self-abnegating career of a foreign missionary.

Outside of this one evening each week in which I gave free rein to my "baby-girl" proclivities, however, I continued to be a most industrious collegian, even winning prizes because of my excelling all others in some branches. My every-day circle had no suspicion of the double life I was leading. Whenever returning home after an evening passed as a fairie, I took the most extreme precautions that I should not be followed, and of course concealed from all who knew me as "Jennie June" that I was a person of more than a common-school education.

All classes of sporting men—young actors, professional gamblers, racetrack bookmakers, and adolescents of some means and without occupation other than to sip continually of all the gross pleasures of life—constituted the associates of "Jennie June" during the following year and a half. I read in the newspaper several times that one of my paramours held a world's record in one branch of sport. I found that very few of this moneyed, sporting class cared to go beyond joking with me and teasing me, and none beyond the age of twenty-five ever went to extremes. In this neighborhood at that time female filles de joie were numerous, and the sporting men were more than satiated. The fairie's success is inversely proportional to unmarried adolescents' opportunities with the gentle sex.

About the beginning of my 14th Street career as a high-class fairie, I removed all the growth of hair on my body and limbs by means of a safety razor so that they were as glabrous as statuary. I considered that I thus beautified my body. The operation had to be repeated about once every two months. I would let the hair on the face grow for a full week, remaining in my room continuously the final two days, Saturday and Sunday, because of my untidy appearance. I would then pull it all out by the roots through the application of depilatory wax. For two or three weeks subsequently my face would be as devoid of hair as any woman's, when the new growth would reach the surface of the skin. After another week's growth, it was necessary to repeat the operation. I had hoped that the repeated violence to the hair-cells would destroy their functioning and I would be permanently rid of facial hair, my most detested mark of the male, but there was no appreciable effect. I also feared the repeated operation might occasion a malignant growth, but I was ready to take every risk.

About the age of seventeen, I was horrified at the first appearance of hair on my face. For several months I refused to shave, but pulled the hairs out when they became long enough to grasp between the fleshy part of the thumb and the blade of a dull knife. I was again horrified when my father presented me with a safety razor. Fortunately for me, this invention shortly preceded my arrival at puberty, my horror of it being far less than of the old-fashioned kind.

During this period of my career, I learned that fairies are maintained in some public houses of the better class, and met several of these refined professionals, who resembled myself both physically and psychically. They commonly have plates substituted for their front teeth. Even I took this expedient under consideration. It was suggested to me to become an inmate of such a house, but I could make the career of a fille de joie only a side issue. I gave first place to the intellectual and others of the highest aims of life. My sister courtesans, both male and female, thought only of the sensual, and had adopted their occupation as a gainful one, whereas I sought merely the satisfaction of strong instincts, which unsatisfied would make practically impossible the higher life I regularly lived.

During this period I knowingly encountered the first case of gonorrhea in a companion. Until eleven years later, when I contracted syphilis, I had an unreasonable horror of venereal disease because of what I had heard in personal purity lectures to students. Nevertheless I was ready to take every risk for the satisfaction of my craving. For my entire open career of twelve years as a fairie—for I did not happen to contract syphilis until its very close—I conceived that in buccal syphilis, the buccal cavity is completely filled with burning, excruciatingly painful ulcers, and no solid nourishment can be taken. A lay confidant almost at the beginning of my fairie days had told me he had seen such a case in a hospital—probably fabricating in order to scare me away from the indulgence of my proclivities. When I finally did contract buccal syphilis I found it not even one-thousandth as serious as it had been represented to me. (See events of 1905.) I always rinsed the buccal cavity as soon as possible subsequently to fellatio, and always kept my system entirely free from alcohol and other narcotics. Throughout my twelve years' association with young men who drank habitually, I always totally abstained from and abhorred alcoholic beverages. So far as I know, I did not contract gonorrhea until 1917, after twenty-four years of promiscuity with the exception of several periods of abstinence or of monandry each of several months duration.

In the ninth year of promiscuity, several long slender venereal warts grew downward from the inside of the upper lip, not visible on the exterior, but troubling me somewhat in articulation. A surgeon excised them and they never returned. In the twelfth year, a large wart appeared just outside the sphincter anus and disappeared without any treatment about twenty months later. I have here indicated all my personal experience with venereal diseases.

In my approximately sixteen hundred intimacies with about eight hundred different companions, I found only about three cases of venereal warts, and about the same number of cases of chancre. Only one confessed to having gonorrhea, and I myself detected it by the discharge on only one other. Young men suffering from syphilis or gonorrhea in membro virili who have a conscience are not likely to permit fellatio. I have, however, encountered the superstition that if a man afflicted with venereal disease can secure fellatio, the malady is imbibed out of the system.

I encountered only four or five monorchids, about five cases of pronounced varicocele, and about five bad cases of phimosis. Slight phimosis was often encountered. I would never have gone to extremes with a monorchid or with one suffering from a bad phimosis if I could have avoided disappointing him or hurting his feelings; and even regretted being thrown with one with only slight phimosis. I was attracted only ad glandem magnam atque de more nudatam. I never encountered a case of hypospade, of epispade, or of noticeably short frenum. Only about four were absolutely incapable of orgasm in my presence, while perhaps two dozen out of the eight hundred found it dilatory or incomplete. With myself orgasm was practically always prompt and complete, but was disagreeable. About a dozen cum orgasmo perfecto non potuerunt ejaculari. Alii duodecim habuerunt tres ejaculationes in semihora.

Solum circiter triginta voluerunt duo aut tres eadem nocte, atque nemo plus. In ninety-five percent of cases, incubuimus solum from twenty to thirty minutes. I never took the initiative in parting, although I was generally quite reconciled. Even in the less than five percent of cases where we passed the night in the same house, I nearly always— because of my inability to fall asleep otherwise—occupied a separate bed except for one hour after retiring and another hour prior to rising.

To return to the events of my Fourteenth Street days, I would sometimes, in the public parlors of the houses of assignation in that vicinity, be a member of a jolly party of adolescents and filles de joie. Everybody would be exceedingly kind and courteous to me, and in general displayed toward one another the most extreme politeness. I have never been in a more charming circle, and would experience the highest earthly bliss. The young men would hold me on their laps and fondle me before the eyes of all, even of strange parties of patrons who were simultaneously occupying the large parlors or drinking saloons. I feared some member of these other parties might recognize me. Occasionally we repaired to a private chamber. In my fairie apprenticeship and during my career around the military posts, I was the financier. But during the present period, that function fell entirely to my associates.

On other occasions, my associates were boisterous and outrageously indecent in their conduct toward me in the public parlors. The following are quotations from my journal: "I have to weep when I reflect that I, a scholar, a litterateur, and a philosopher, am so often made the sport and laughing-stock of the immoral and godless crowd which assembles in the parlor of the X—— Hotel. To think of my acting like a simpleton, and being looked upon as a simpleton by those greatly inferior to me in mental ability!"

"I am satiated with sensual pleasure. It is the vanity of vanities. Good deeds done our fellow men are the best investment in life. I pray God to send forth laborers into His harvest, and to let me be one. When I see the multitude of young people wandering astray, as sheep without a shepherd, the words of scripture ring through my ears, 'Comfort ye, comfort ye, my people!' Sometimes I seem to have a clairvoyant vision into the future, and behold myself, finally saved from animality, commissioned by the great I AM to be a proclaimer of the blessed Gospel of peace and good will among men."

O ne evening a strange adolescent accosted me on the street: "You are a fairie, aren't you?"

"What makes you think so?"

"No one but a fairie would stare at a fellow like you do. Don't you want to take a walk with me over to the East River?" (Where the streets were entirely deserted at night.)

On the way he inquired my real name, occupation, residence, and all about me, and feigned a friendly interest. I of course gave false answers. Arrived in the deserted region, he allowed me to incriminate myself for a single second. Then he seized me violently and exclaimed: "I was just laying for fellows like you. You have been lying to me. You don't live down on the Bowery, and you are no tailor. I know you! I have seen you uptown! Now I have evidence against you! That is all I was after! I am a detective, and you are under arrest!"

"What have I done to you that you should treat me like this? I did not accost you! You accosted me! Have mercy on me, a poor unfortunate, and let me go!"

As we walked along, I, unexpectedly to him, wrenched myself from his grip and escaped. A kind Providence made me unusually fleet of foot, and many times in my subsequent career, I outran a persecutor. The young man may have been fabricating, but detectives have been actually sent out by the authorities to entrap inverts. The author knows of a case where the invert was induced by the detective to incriminate himself where he could be photographed in the act, and as a result spent several years in state's prison.

On another warm evening, I was skylarking with several high-class adolescents in the deserted region in question. A gang of youthful dockrats surprised us, and we fled in a panic. I happened to be captured. Having perceived that I was an invert, they at first conducted themselves in what was to me the most pleasing manner and then robbed me.

One of my associates on a summer evening conducted me to Stuyvesant Square, a few blocks from my usual haunts, and introduced me to his circle of friends, who in good weather spent part of nearly every evening on the park benches. All these adolescents were members of a young men's club in the neighborhood, with about three score members of which I soon became acquainted. Morally and religiously, these young men stood higher than any other class that I ever associated with as "Jennie June." No virile young men in New York City stand higher than they, being of the best "Y. M. C. A. type." In summer, for about ten years subsequently, I occasionally called on my many friends some of whom were almost sure to be seated in this small park during part of a pleasant evening. I saw some successively reach puberty, young manhood, marriage, and fatherhood.

The majority of this superior class of young men treated me kindly, but only about one in eight ever went to extremes, and these never more than six times individually. A considerable proportion of those who knew me to be a fairie, however, thought I must therefore be a monster of wickedness, and of the many different sets of adolescents with whom I associated as "Jennie June," only one other inflicted on me as much suffering as did this Stuyvesant Square group. An extenuating circumstance is that I could not let them know that I was a person of strong religious and moral convictions, and habitually led a respectable life. I was always entirely inoffensive, merely coquetting with those to whom I had been introduced. My influence on their lives was not at all bad. I even encouraged them to live the higher Christian life, as about one-half were church members, and practically all, regular attendants on its services.

Some of their number who looked upon a fairie as necessarily a monster of wickedness—for why otherwise would the law place upon his sexual conduct a penalty of ten years in state's prison?—gave me several severe thrashings, so that I always visited the Square in great fear, but took the risk for the affection that I had for those who were glad to have me talk and coquet with them.

The following was my extreme suffering at their hands: I happened to be one evening seated alone on a park bench. Several of my enemies discovered and surrounded me. Very much frightened I attempted to leave, but they would not permit it. They stuck pins into me, inflicted slight burns with lighted matches, and pinched me unmercifully, particularly the penis. There were policemen within hailing distance, but I was told I would be arrested if I called for help. I was entirely innocent, but the police would have believed the false testimony against me of a half dozen accusers. When satisfied with wreaking their vengeance, they turned me over to a policeman with charges, but he simply ordered me out of the park. Seemingly the higher the standard of morality of adolescents as at present trained, the greater the physical violence that they inflict on fairies. One lecturer to students on personal purity whom I heard counselled his adolescent hearers to give a blow in the face to any associate who ever suggested homosexuality.

I wish here to emphasize the fact that there would be no risk of the spread of homosexual practices through the removal of the legal penalties attached to them and the consequent removal, at least in large part, of the practice of our best adolescents in beating up and torturing androgynes because the latter are outlaws. Almost exclusively, those addicted by birth to these relations—regarded by the normal males as highly unaesthetic—and largely irresponsible for their conduct, can alone occasion these so-called "crimes." What is the use then of laws against practices really harmless to society and to the adolescent—while perhaps harmful to the invert to the same degree that marital relations are harmful to a wife and mother—and occasioned alone by those who are driven by an innate impulse, often uncontrollable? The law does not imprison deaf-mutes for being born with abnormal inner ears, and why should it imprison members of this other congenitally defective class? The invert asks only for the same standing before the law accorded all other men. But as law and custom always make special exemptions for the congenitally defective, perhaps it would be right to show special mercy to the invert.

One evening at the close of about eighteen months of my avocation as a Fourteenth Street "street-walker," I was promenading up and down. Now and then some habitue of the district would recognize me, stop, and flirt for a few minutes. Finally I encountered a party of six adolescents. Four had never met me previously, yet all talked in a most free and unrestrained, as well as indecent manner. After a while, one proposed that I accompany him to his room.

"I am afraid those other fellows will follow us and hurt me."

"They are all friends of yours."

"I am not so sure about that. You know some fellows hate a fairie, and some of those boys appear very heartless. You saw how rough they were to me right on the street! If they should try to hurt me, would you fight for me?"

"Of course."

"How could you alone fight against five fellows?"

"Well, I would do the best I could, and depend on you to help me."

"Don't think of depending on me. You know a girl can't fight. All a girl can do when fellows fight is to look on."

"You could at least scream, couldn't you?"

"Yes, I could scream."

"Well, you do the screaming, and I'll do the fighting."

A few minutes after we arrived in the young man's quarters in a furnished-room house, the other five burst in. They proved to be as heartless a gang as I had ever met, although belonging to the prosperous class of society. Micturiverunt super meis vestibus atque me coegerunt facere rem mihi horribilissimam (balneum ani cum lingua, non aliter quam meretrices faciunt). Me coegerunt recipere tres eodem tempore, fellatio, paedicatio, atque manustupratio. Ultimum mihi imperatum cum adolescens non potuit facere inter femora eodem tempore. Later one who had difficulty in achieving the desired results me coegit ad fellationem unam semihoram continuously, repeatedly punching me in the head and face because I did not do better by him. Again for a half hour continuously me coegerunt ut supinum cubem atque usi erunt ore meo sicuti cunno, sic me strangulantes horribiliter. Cum priapus concurreret meas dentes, they would punch me in the face, atque mandabant ut desisterem eos mordere.

This was one of my three very worst experiences of sexual abuse. The physical suffering and discomfort were extreme, but I was so fascinated by the savagery and the beauty of my tormentors that I experienced a species of mental satisfaction, being willing to suffer death if only I could contribute to their pleasure. During my career I had numerous experiences, but much less trying, along this same line. A fairie is often thus treated by cruel, lecherous adolescents, since they know he is an outlaw and can not bring them to justice.

Their lechery finally satiated, one of them stuck a handkerchief into my mouth, and said: "Do you know you are worse than a hog? You d—— fairie, going around to corrupt young fellows! We will teach you to keep away from Fourteenth Street hereafter!" Another cried: "You've got to let me have first whack at him!"

I was conducted to a dark, deserted street, where one of them rained violent blows in my face, while I did nothing except to seek to protect my features as much as possible with my hands. Finally it occurred to me to feign unconsciousness—my first adoption of this ruse—when they all hurried away.

Only through the special mercy of an overruling Providence I was saved from permanent injury that night, and on several other subsequent nights of my career as a fairie. During my Mulberry Street career I never received the least blow, and during my years of association with hundreds of soldiers of four forts, I never received a blow deserving of mention. But I was seriously assaulted three times by soldiers of a fifth fort, several times by Stuyvesant Square acquaintances, several times by acquaintances of my Bowery period, and only the one time just described, by Fourteenth Street acquaintances. A certain class of adolescents, regarding the conduct of a fairie as the depth of depravity, yearn to lay violent hands on him.

I was compelled immediately after the assault described to have my wounds dressed by a physician. On subsequently arriving in my room, I followed my universal custom after a return from a female-impersonation spree: that is, the first thing I did was to fall on my knees and thank the Omnipresent, All-pervading Spirit, that I had been permitted to see home again and resume for a season the ordinary course of my life as a scholar. But after retiring, I could not sleep, but tossed about all night in a half-waking delirium. Every moment it seemed as if I would become a raving maniac. I moaned repeatedly, and called upon God to show mercy and deliver me from my mental agony.

Is it just that inoffensive inverts should be subjected to such outrages, and have no redress? A confidant, with whom I discussed proceedings against these conscienceless young men, gave it as his opinion that the court would immediately turn around and make me—who, if I must say it myself, have always been unusually conscientious notwithstanding my sensuality—the defendant against the most serious charges. (This practically happened in 1905.) What other class of men is treated thus by the law and public opinion?

The reader may reply: "If they don't want to suffer in this way, let them stay home and keep away from people who deal thus with them." But inverts often have to follow their own nature, although they have striven hard to act according to the nature of the majority of men. With the present organization of society, and the present extreme scorn manifested toward victims of inversion, it is only natural, and almost necessary, if inverts desire to preserve the respect of their every-day circles, that they should visit incognito some section of a great city remote from their own. Suppose in a war between two tribes of red men, a brave is captured, consigned to adopt the dress and occupation of a squaw, and is in every way treated as a squaw. Would this unnatural life be to the brave's tastes? Would he be blamed if he sought to escape where he could live according to his masculine inclinations? No more is the passive invert to be blamed for escaping occasionally where he can live according to his quasi-feminine instincts.

The remedy lies in the dissemination of just and correct views of inversion, the removal of the deepseated but ill founded prejudice against individuals thus marked by Nature which is regnant in all classes of society, and the repeal of the unjustified laws against inverts, which more than anything else account for the unthinking man's persecution of these stepchildren of Nature. Then like the red-man androgyne, his cultured counterpart can, without losing his economic and social position, choose a mate from among his every-day circle. As long as he is outwardly modest and chaste, he should receive only commiseration and condonation for his homosexuality.

For a week following the assault described, my terribly disfigured face confined me to my room. When somewhat healed, I was compelled to give my every-day circle a false explanation. For several weeks I felt only hatred for all adolescent libertines. At the end of that period I chanced to witness a youthful artilleryman reeling around a ferry waiting-room. Fascinated, I entered into conversation, told him I was an invert, and requested quasi-permanent monandry. His exact words were: "With all my heart."

I began to frequent one evening a week the fort where he was stationed, but we disclosed to no one that I was other than an ordinary young man. I was, moreover, so fascinated with him that I did not seriously consider flirtation with his comrades. We exchanged numerous passionate love letters—my first essay in this field. I was also now inspired to compose my first amatory ballads, which were in praise of my "Man behind the guns," and transmitted to him.

Our intimacy continued for several months, until, having become an outcast and penniless, I was unable to make him presents, and he consequently became negligent in keeping his appointments.

During this year 1896, I read Krafft-Ebing's "Psychopathia-Sexualis," besides a number of articles on inversion which had been published in American and European journals. I availed myself of the library of the New York Acadamy of Medicine. Some years later I read there Havelock Ellis's "Sexual Inversion."

This autobiography has now reached my twenty-third year. I had received my baccalaureate degree with honors, and was in my second year of graduate study. I had not really degenerated morally or religiously. For the entire year ending at the date at which I had now arrived, the aggregate time devoted to female impersonation and coquetry was approximately one hundred hours, as compared with about twenty-one hundred devoted to my studies and two hundred and fifty to the worship of my Creator and religious culture. Surely I was not to be tabooed as a moral leper. While the average church member, through lack of understanding of the conditions surrounding my life, would have branded me as a hypocrite, I sincerely believed and lived up to the fundamental truths of the Christian religion.

I still enjoyed an unblemished reputation. I associated with all my beaux, including my soldier friend, incognito. Always on returning home after an evening passed as "Jennie June," I took precautions that I was not followed.

The wreck of my happy and highly successful student-career was now brought about by a physician whom I had consulted in hope of a cure for my inversion, but not one of the two gentlemen already named. He happened to number the president of the university among his friends, and whispered to him that I ought not to be continued as a student. I was immediately expelled.

I earned my living in a minor capacity in the university, and expulsion also meant that my income was cut off. The shock of expulsion rendered me a mental wreck. But I did not have the courage to return to my village home. Nor could I even apply to my father for money. Since soon after my arrest two years prior to the present date, he had, as already described, displayed a pronounced antipathy for me, rendering my visits home almost intolerable. In addition, because of the double-life my nature forced me to lead, I decided I must remain in New York.

I removed to a part of the city where I would not be likely to encounter any of my college acquaintances, and began to look around for means of support. I spent several hours every day in answering advertisements. I would have been only too glad to accept such a position as shoveling coal into a furnace, but at the end of a month, had found nothing. In applying for positions, I was abashed in the consciousness that I was ranked as a degenerate and an outcast from society. I could not name as reference any member of the university or let it become known that I had been a student there. After my expulsion I called on the two professors with whom I was most intimate, and asked if I could refer to them. One replied: "Knowing your nature, I could not recommend you for any position, however menial. You cannot be trusted." (And yet shortly afterward I was for thirty months in the employ of a millionaire in the most confidential capacity, and was surpassed in faithfulness by no employee.) The other: "You must realize that you are an outcast from society."

All hope for the future and all courage for battling with the world were gone, and every day on my return from several hours' fruitless search, I would throw myself on the bed and give vent to my feelings in a violent fit of weeping. While walking the street, I would weep aloud and be on the borderline of hysterical screaming. I repeatedly entertained thoughts of suicide.

In a few weeks I was penniless and a shelterless wanderer on the streets in midwinter. I was driven for shelter to the Bowery, because there alone lodging could be obtained for fifteen cents, and a big meal of coarse and even disgusting food for ten cents. Thus I was compelled to live for nine weeks before a way was opened to something better.

During the nine weeks I was of the opinion that I must pass the rest of my days as an outcast from society, while of course living out the "Jennie-June" life to which I was apparently predestined. I was grateful to Providence that it was I and not one of my sisters who was predetermined to the life of a fille de joie and an outcast. In suffering such a fate, I believed that I was paying the penalty to God for the sin of some progenitor. I believed myself appointed by the God who visits the iniquities of the fathers upon the children to live out the rest of my life in mourning and paroxysms of grief, such as then visited me every day.

The manner of life of a high-class fairie has been described. I was fated also to trace out the life of a low-class one. But even in my present extreme poverty, I was decidedly averse to making a gainful occupation out of the life. I wanted my freedom of action, and was unalterably opposed to intimacy for pecuniary gain with any one whom I did not adore. During the present nine weeks I accepted whatever was voluntarily proffered, but otherwise left money entirely out of consideration. I moreover did not resume my Fourteenth Street life, which might have proved less impecunious, because it was comparatively "poor pickings" there; because I was much more strongly attracted toward the rough, burly adolescents of the foreign laborer quarters than toward the young gentleman libertines of Fourteenth Street; and finally because I had twice encountered on Fourteenth Street associates at the university. Fortunately I happened to be alone both times and my actions not suspicious, but I realized I was taking a great deal of risk there. Moreover, I did not return regularly to my Mulberry Street friends because I now found on my occasional visits there that it was a barren "stamping ground." The tradition was lodged there that I was well furnished with money, which reputation is fatal to the success of a penniless fairie.

Living as I was now compelled to live and necessarily mingling daily with men of loose morals, the charm of masculine beauty proved more powerful than ever before. Furthermore, it is not surprising that a person, deprived of even what are regarded as the necessities of a decent existence, should indulge immoderately in the single one of life's pleasures of which there was an abundant supply. In the environment in which forces outside of my control placed me, there was in me a practically irresistible impulse to adopt the manner of life I did. I would never have made the profession of the fairie the main business of life if it had not been for the peculiar concurrence of circumstances, expulsion from college, inability to find respectable employment, etc. That I now led the life I did was perhaps more the fault of Christian society than my own. While the world condemned, I have always believed that the Omniscient Judge pardoned because I was the victim of circumstances and of innate psychical forces.

The fact that I could now satisfy every day my instinctive yearnings to pass for a female and spend six evenings a week in the company of adolescent ruffians went far towards counterbalancing the many tears I had to shed when there was nothing to divert my thoughts from my condition of an outcast and an outlaw. I never coquetted on Sunday evenings, which I devoted to worship of my Creator at some mission. I no longer experienced any shame at displaying my feminine mentality everywhere outside of the missions, as no one knew who I was. In many neighborhoods I was hailed as "Jennie June."

Besides the Bowery, the streets most frequented by me during these nine weeks—as well as during the not immediately following two years when I was compelled to go on a female-impersonation spree once in two weeks—were the following: (1) In the foreign Hebrew quarter: Grand, from Bowery eastward to Allen, and Allen and Christie, for several blocks on both sides of Grand. (2) In the foreign Italian quarter, containing also a large sprinkling of Irish immigrants: Grand, from Bowery westward to Sullivan and Thompson; the whole lengths of the two latter streets; Bleecker from Thompson to Carmine; and Mulberry south of Spring. (3) In Chinatown: Doyers, Pell, and Mott streets. I did not seek the Chinese, who were sexually repulsive, but the adolescent toughs and young gentleman libertines who visited Chinatown evenings from all parts of the city.

The present palatial Police Headquarters, built subsequently to my frequenting these neighborhoods, is at the geographical center of my field of those days. My fairie apprenticeship was in large part passed within two hundred feet of the site of this edifice, then occupied by a public market, and some of my fairie adventures occurred on the very site.

With the exception of the soldiers and sailors, practically all my beaux of these neighborhoods were of foreign parentage, but born in New York. The Irish predominated, then came the Italians, and then the Hebrews. Practically all belonged to one of these classes, as did nearly all the inhabitants of the quarters frequented. But my experience as a fairie elsewhere, particularly over a large part of Europe, proved that religion and race make no difference in respect to the reception accorded an invert.

Since I had lost my position in the social body, I was willing to take greater risks of bodily harm. I would enter low "clubrooms" with several wild heartless ruffians whom perhaps I had never seen before. Many a midnight I was promenading the street arm in arm with a pair of adolescent longshoremen cutthroats whom I had never seen before, or with youthful soldiers or sailors. Even some youthful policemen went skylarking with me on the back streets after all the inhabitants had gone to bed. Most of the police on the Bowery knew me as a fairie, but were always friendly. This street at that time was the wide-open "red-light" district for the un-Americanized laborer and for the common soldier or sailor.

When I felt feeble and fatigued—then my usual condition—flirtation quickened the heart's action and the flow of blood. I forgot my weariness, and if shivering with the cold before, my body now glowed with warmth.

Incorrigible thieves, who had only just learned that I was a fairie, have immediately grasped me on a brightly lighted street thronged with pedestrians, and ransacked my pockets, while clasping me to their breast and crying out: "Oh how she loves me! Oh how she loves me!" Their purpose was to create the impression on those who were hurrying by that I was embracing them. Some adolescent ruffians demanded money every time they ran across me, and helped themselves to all I had if I refused them. If they found nothing, they would sometimes beat me in their disappointment. Some would promise me a beating when we next met unless I brought them a stipulated sum.

Occasionally boys hardly in their teens would demand blackmail. I was entirely innocent of even carrying on conversation with them, but they knew me through the adolescents of their neighborhood. The charges of these mere boys, though entirely false, were feared much more than those of adults, because it would have been a far more serious offence to have had anything to do with those of tender years. Being no match for me in size, these boys had to resort to various expedients to extort money. They would sometimes attack me five or six together. Words cannot depict my terror on being thus attacked. The boys had their parents near to take their part, while I had not a soul to appeal to for help and to establish my innocence. I feared that all the ignorant foreign population would rise up against me, and in their wrath, kill me.

If a mere boy attacked me single-handed, he would suddenly leap upon my back, hold himself there by throwing one arm tight around my neck so that I could not dislodge him, and if I ran, had to carry him along; and with the hand that was free, he would rain blows on me. To escape from such a predicament, I was glad to give him a few nickels.

Naturally as timid as the cry-baby species of woman, I always promenaded the dimly lighted side streets of these foreign quarters like a cat crossing a road, ever alert, ever halting to reconnoitre, and occasionally compelled to take to my heels on catching sight of the burly form, a dozen yards away, of a ruffian who never cared for my society, but who, because of innate loathing of a fairie—nourished by the statutes' making the latter an outlaw—beat and robbed me at every opportunity. It was similar with young men not attractive to me, to whom I had refused my company. Through being as swift of foot as a gazelle, I escaped many blows. If flight were impossible, I would try entreaty. If entreaty failed, I would resort to ruse. Knocked down by a sledge-hammer blow, I would feign insensibility, and in all but one instance that ended the beating.

Is it any wonder that generally before starting out for a ramble on the side streets, I felt as if I were going forth to meet death on the scaffold? But I was fascinated by the adolescents who spent their evenings on these streets, and who had previously given me their company, and I was hoping to meet them again. I was also led on by the craze for as many as possible every evening. Maximum erat octo; modus, duo aut tres.

On the Bowery itself, soldiers and sailors were my special quest. As already indicated, these two types were to me the *beau ideal* of masculine beauty. I outline one of my most successful nights.

I encounter four stalwart artillerymen of about my own age. I am bewitched and must find some way to make their acquaintance immediately. I would not take the risk of indecently accosting them as girls commonly did on the Bowery at that time. I adopted the expedient of walking along under their noses on the crowded sidewalk, swaying my shoulders energetically and taking very short steps. In a few seconds they shouted out, "Hello Pretty!" surrounded me, and overwhelmed me with terms of endearment, while I begged them to take me to be their baby and slave. A room is secured for an hour. When the time came to part, I was pained at the thought. It was hard for a moment or an hour to possess the society of a human demigod whom one would like to abide with and worship and serve forever, and then to be abruptly, completely, and eternally separated. Returned to the street, they repeatedly request me to leave them. Arrived at their objective, a low dance-hall, they are compelled to use threats of violence, and abandon me at the entrance.

Two flashily dressed adolescents emerge. They halt in order to light cigarettes but find they have no matches. I offer some, welcoming the opportunity to enter into conversation. "You are handsome, sporty-looking fellows. I cannot tell you how much I adore you."

"What's here? A fairie?"

"Yes, I'm a fairie, and I would like to be a slave to sports like you. Don't this fellow look every inch a slugger? How I worship sluggers!"

"You do, do you? Do you want to take a walk with us?"

"Delighted. I was just crying because some soldiers shook me, but making your acquaintance brings me happiness again, because you are wild young bloods."

"What do you see in a fellow to love any way? I don't see anything. What good do you get out of loving a fellow?"

"Well, what do you see in a girl to love? I don't see anything. Girls are not brave. They are not rough. They are not strong. You are brave, rough, and strong, and that is why I love you. I love fellows for the same reason you love girls—because they are my opposites. The weak love the strong and the strong, the weak. The brave love the timid and the timid, the brave. The shy love the bold and the bold, the shy.

I love a boy
Because I'm coy;
It would be wrong
Not to love the strong;

> *In the fierce and rough*
> *I find the right stuff;*
> *The gallant and brave*
> *They make me rave;*
> *While the reckless and bold*
> *Are better than gold."*

I always sought by sprightly conversation to win the good-will of chance companions, but a small proportion were incorrigible. As soon as we arrived on a dark deserted street, one of the young men said: "Do you know I am a detective, and I arrest you for accosting us. But if you'll hand me a dollar, I will let you off this time." (Impersonating a detective is a common practice in robbing fairies.)

"I haven't that much, and you wouldn't take from a poor unfortunate the few cents he has, would you?"

"Hand over all you've got! You'll find you have run up against a hard party!"

"You ought not to hit me like that, because I'm a girl. A fellow ought to be ashamed to hit a girl."

"You're no girl, you!" adding the appropriate vulgar epithet.

"I am too. I can take you to a doctor and prove it by his word. I am a girl incarnated in a boy's body."

For fear of a pummeling, I handed over all I had, less than a dollar.

"I am undecided what to do with you, lock you up, or give you a thrashing, you d—— fairie!"

"Please let me go! I am very weak and can't stand much. You want to punish me for being a fairie, but I can't help being what Nature made me. Do you think any one would be a fairie from choice when they are the most despised of mankind? Think how much better God has been to you than to me. Have pity on me! I am one of the most unfortunate of human beings! For your dear mother's sake—whom every boy must love—I beg you to show me mercy!"

An appeal to mother-love seldom failed. I return to the dance-hall and enter. My soldier friends are nowhere to be seen, so I take a seat among a group of blue-jackets of my own age, and am not slow in betraying my character through expressions of my admiration. A room is hired.

It was after three A.M. when I sought rest. But my brain was so excited that I tossed about for two hours, having alternately chills for five minutes, and then fever. I felt that I was going to lose my mind any moment, and besought the Omniscient to allay my excitement. I had gone beyond my strength, and in addition the excessive venery was harmful to the nervous system. After five o'clock, I repeatedly fell into a doze, but immediately beginning to dream that my face and buccal cavity were covered with the most loathsome syphilitic ulcers—such as a university confidant had once told me he had seen in a hospital, *falsely*, in order to scare me from fellatio with strangers—I would awake with a start, horror-stricken. After suffering this nightmare a dozen times, I finally fell into a restful sleep lasting until early afternoon.

A typical night on the side streets: On Canal Street near Thompson was a pool parlor where acquaintances of the highest type for this period of my life—in large part adolescent drivers for the express companies—passed their evenings. While I was received in pool parlors of a lower grade, my presence would have been unwelcome here. One evening I was loafing in front of the place, waiting for some acquaintance to pass. Before long I was recognized, my presence announced to those within, and all temporarily interrupted their games to crowd around me. The majority had never seen me before, and were anxious to interview the person who was then the talk of the young "sports" of that part of the town, as well as of many other parts. Even in the foreign-laborer quarters of New York City, it is rare for a young man to run across a professional fairie—as they constitute as near as I can *guess* only one out of every three thousand physical males—and furthermore, I have been repeatedly told that I acted the part in such perfection as never seen in any other.

Question after question was addressed to me: How did I ever get it into my head that I was a girl? Why had I been born that way? Was it because my parents had indulged shortly before I was born, so that membrum virile concurreret meam faciem? Wasn't it because God wished to visit upon me some sin of my parents? (Practically all were more or less devout Roman Catholics.) Were any of my brothers similarly affected? Had I ever had relations with a woman? At what age did the peculiar desire show itself? Etc. I gladly answered every question, and told them the story of my life, only with such non-essential variations from the truth as my protection demanded.

All soon returned to their games except four, none of whom I had ever met previously. I consented to take a walk with two, and insisted that the others must leave us because of their age, only sixteen. We strolled to the neighboring absolutely deserted shore of the Hudson River, and took possession of one of the hundreds of covered trucks stalled there for the night. I soon discovered the two that had been left behind peeking into the van. Startled for fear of a plot, I leaped to the ground in order to flee. But on their immediately starting in to caress me, I fell at their feet in adoration. Both were clad in the blue uniform of express-company employees, and therefore presented a particularly pleasing appearance.

Some adolescents—as these four—went to extremes just for the novelty of it, out of curiosity to observe my peculiar nature, or to derive amusement through frolicking with me. In some cases, subsequently filled with abhorrence that I would so lower myself—as they looked upon it—they would be moved to inflict physical pain, or temporary disfigurement of the face, which I shrunk from a thousand times more than from pain.

After an hour of such treatment as filled me with bliss, a change of attitude began to manifest itself. Knowing by experience that I was destined to suffer, I watched my chance, unexpectedly dashed away from them, and with the extraordinary speed that I was capable of when frightened, directed my course away from the absolutely deserted river front. All four immediately started in pursuit. The zig-zag chase—for I turned at every corner—extended more than a quarter of a mile. The terrifying shouts, "Stop thief! Stop thief!" rang in my ears throughout the course, and I as continuously prayed for the help of the Almighty to enable me to escape. Their cries, however, failed to bring assistance since the streets of this wholesale and warehouse section are at midnight entirely deserted.

I was at about the end of my endurance, and realized that unless something unexpected happened, I must in a moment fall into their hands. But a merciful Providence was about to intervene to save a persecuted outcast from what promised to be a serious assault. I had just turned the acute angle that Vestry Street makes with Canal, and the nearest of my pursuers was only a hundred feet behind. Toward midnight the horse cars on Canal Street ran only at fifteen minute intervals, but at that very second one happened to be jogging along only twenty-five feet from the apex of the acute angle. I leaped upon the platform and entered the car. If this had happened in sight of my pursuers, they would undoubtedly have followed my example and assaulted me inside the car, as happened in another similar adventure.

On another midnight, as I was sauntering down—looking for company, I became infatuated with a giant of a ruffian seated on a hydrant just below—Street. I began my prattle and we soon walked off together to the neighboring—Park. He appeared to be such a reckless character that I was afraid to accompany him off a public place, and contented myself with spooning on one of the park benches. We were soon joined by two pals, who had followed to see what was up, because maybe there was a chance for highway robbery. But they discovered that it was only a low-class fairie. They were also splendid specimens of the youthful ruffian. I was madly attracted toward all three, and now reclining in the bosom of one, and now in that of another, I gave utterance to the infant's natural language expressive of contentment at being petted and babied by these giants, whom I affectionately called my "Big Braves." I would lift their hands to my mouth and cover them with kisses, and roll up their sleeves and cover their arms with kisses.

After some time, two of them said goodnight, leaving me alone with the giant whose acquaintance I had first made. I finally agreed to accompany him to his room. Whenever we sighted a policeman, he remarked: "Let's go over to the other side of the street. I don't want that cop to see my face." After entering the side-door of a repulsive-looking "Saloon," we walked down a very long passage, divided into sections by several heavily barricaded doors, each provided with a peep-hole and door-tender, who opened only to the elect. Protection was thus secured again surprises by the police. We finally arrived in a spacious room filled with small tables, around which were seated a dozen flashily dressed "sports," about the same number of shabbily clad ruffians, three or four girls costumed as for a fancy-dress ball, and five "sports" in the biological sense of that word, that is, youths with no front teeth, hair à la mode de Oscar Wilde (that is, hanging down in ringlets over the ears and collar) and clad in bright colored wrappers. Their faces were painted, and their bodies also were seen to be when later they threw aside the loose wrappers.

The assemblage were sipping their favorite beverages. From time to time decidedly obscene dances took place—in 1897 to be seen only in brothels, but in 1917 gracing even university receptions. In the terpsichorean art, our universities today stand only where our brothels stood twenty years ago. One of the painted youths furnished the dance music. Another from time to time rendered the latest songs in a treble voice.

When some came forward to make my acquaintance, my friend introduced me as "Miss June." I protested: "Not Miss June. That doesn't sound pretty. Jennie June. I am only a baby-girl, not a grown-up female."

Three of the fairies were introduced to me as Jersey Lily, Annie Laurie, and Grace Darling. Two others had adopted the names of living star actresses. The unreflecting and uneducated victims of innate androgynism, and having passed their lives exclusively in the slums of New York, they had always been perfectly satisfied with the lot Nature had ordained for them. As already stated, in unenlightened lands, as India, these human "sports," clad in feminine apparel, appear in public in the company of young bloods. Among the American Indians, they adopt the dress and occupation of squaws, become married to a brave, and lead a quiet virtuous life of toil. But Christendom has refused to acknowledge that God has created this type of human being, the woman with masculine genitals. It hunts them down, and drives them from one section of our great cities to another by repeated raids on their resorts. It attributes their fundamental peculiarities to moral degradation, when they are due to Nature. Of course, in the case of these fairies in the slums of New York, deep moral degradation had supervened upon their innate androgynism.

Active pederasts, who frequent such resorts, and normal young men who visit them just to see life, spoon with me. A charming smooth-spoken young gallant holds me on his lap before the roomful of people, and addresses me as "My dear boy," to which I reply, "Please don't call me *boy;* call me *girl.*" I am bewitched by my wooer, who uses to me the most indecent language I ever heard, and right in the hearing of all those assembled. I do not act rational. I do not wish to act rational. I wish to act like a baby girl. I am in high spirits, and the men visitors are much amused at my conduct. The other fairies also impersonate the woman and the baby, much to the amusement of their audience. Whoever has visited such a performance must acknowledge that this type of human being are born actors, or actresses, whichever term may be preferred. They themselves prefer the latter.

On another midnight when I was promenading the Bowery, a band of young desperadoes, who had been indulging freely in liquor, emerged from a dance-hall. They were longshoremen, coal-heavers, etc. Their burly forms and bacchanalian madness fascinated me, and I rushed into their midst exclaiming: "Where did you get these pretty red badges? Won't you give me one?" They were all members of some political club which had given a dance that night.

The gang immediately recognized my character, and I became the recipient of chivalrous and amorous attentions from them all. I accompanied them on their way home, down the Bowery to Chatham Square, and then eastward to the neighborhood of Water Street. They repeatedly urged me to enter some low dive with them, but I would not think of it. They were too reckless and vicious a lot, and I was satisfied with being wooed by them on the public street in their delightfully wild and rough way. Finally arrived at a groggery where some of them felt at home, they will no longer listen to a refusal. They drag me inside and down into the cellar.

Has the reader ever perused the account of the deeds of the sons of Belial in Gibeah, performed 3,400 years ago to the detriment of a certain Levite and his concubine, as recorded in the Book of Judges? These modern sons of Belial, these lowest, most ignorant, most animal, and most vicious of all the inhabitants of the modern Babylon, repeated that night on their helpless victim the deeds of the men of ancient Gibeah. I was then carried to the street and abandoned.

This assault proved to be the millstone that broke the camel's back. I was at last rendered unable to be on my feet owing to spinal trouble, and to excruciating pain in the anus whenever I attempted to walk. I was compelled to enter a hospital.

For several years following, cleanliness required me gerere pannum perpetuo intra subuculam causa incontinentiae defecationis. But it was of little account, by no means rendering me what Beza would denominate "a stinking androgyne." The liquid excretion did not at all interfere with my pursuits of the scholar or the female-impersonator. As I must keep everything secret, I took upon myself the entire care of the cloths in my room. After a few years, the sphincter again functioned completely.

When able to leave the hospital, I felt satiated for life with coitus, and exceedingly homesick. I yielded to the temptation to find shelter under the parental roof. On my arrival home, which I had hardly expected to see again, I could do nothing but weep for the first half hour, and it was several hours before I could speak without bursting into tears. My mother enfolded her "little innocent boy," and my father had softened. Of course I never gave a true account of our period of estrangement.

I now believed that my career as a fairie was over. My early religious enthusiasm was renewed, and I began to spend a large part of my time in related studies. As already made known, I had had the career of a foreign missionary in mind from childhood up to the age of nineteen, and before many weeks I felt that now I was loosed from that terrible obsession by the "procreative" side of human life, I could look forward to laboring in the field of missions. After two months of activity in church work in my native village, an opening presented itself in the near-by metropolis.

I thus passed an exceedingly satisfactory summer, and hoped and prayed that this religious enthusiasm might continue indefinitely. What a contrast between this life and that as Jennie June! While the phenomena of the procreative side of life bring to man the highest earthly bliss, they also occasion the intensest misery. The life as Jennie June had been a bitter life apart from all the extraneous suffering. But in a life given for others, seeking not its own, there was everything satisfying, and nothing to regret. Truly there is a glorious salvation from sin and unhappiness in announcing glad tidings to the poor, binding up the broken-hearted, and opening the eyes of the spiritually blind.

But this salvation was not to be mine. It is in the power of the vast majority of the human race to live what are called decent, moral lives; but it is not in the power of all. My "sin" was a disease of the mind, not wilful sin, especially at this and earlier periods of my career. I was a born "nymphomaniac," if this word may be used of one who has no nymphae. In respect to the strength of the urge after coition, I am akin to the male rather than the female sex. As few others have tried, I tried to overcome the evil inherent in my nature, but in vain. The manner in which this period of religious enthusiasm ended is shown in the following extract from a letter written to my spiritual adviser.

". . . But the blessing of God suddenly left me, and I found myself without a single thought on religion to give expression to. Previously I had no loss for words. Every verse of scripture had been to me a revelation of divine truth, bristling with suggestions for my talks; but now all are to me empty words, without force. The scriptures appear to me false. The story of Christ appears to me to be a myth. I agonize before God, and beseech Him to restore unto me the joy of salvation, and not to take the Holy Spirit from me. I cry out: 'I do not believe it to be a myth! These infidel thoughts which come upon me are not mine! I believe, Lord, I believe, but my mind proves false to me! Help thou mine unbelief!'

"But God makes himself known in no way. It is to me as if there were no God. But I will persist in believing there is one. I read the Bible chapter after chapter, praying for light, but all the time there is nothing but darkness and doubt in my heart. Continually the thought comes into my mind: 'There is no personal God.' I still read diligently Row's 'Jesus of the Evangelists,' which in former times had carried me up into the third heaven of bliss in the conviction of the historic character of the Gospels, and in adoration of the Christ; but the very same book is now tedious and falls flat. I had been speaking as if fully inspired by the Holy Ghost, and lost all consciousness of self. But the last three times, I spoke simply because I had to, my own heart being full of *emotions* of unbelief. After three flat failures, I decided to give up.

"My thorn in the flesh also now gives me no rest day nor night. It drives peace from my mind every day, and sleep from my eyes every night. Few have to endure such torture of unsatisfied longing. How I do bewail the fact that I have this abnormal passion which cries out for appeasement! It is not I who wish the gratification, I call God to witness. I wish all passion annihilated in me, and to spend my days in study and in doing good. . . I have been celibate five months, and expected to continue so forever, but I now suspect such a life to be contrary to God's will. All my hopes of leading an honorable life have been dissipated. All the indications are that God does not call me to preach the Gospel. . ."

A few mornings later I happened to be reading in the 23d Street Y. M. C. A. A poorly clad adolescent brushed lightly against me and I felt myself electrified. Looking up furtively, I recognized a Bowery favorite of six months before. To me his face appeared to be lighted up with an unearthly radiance, and a halo of glory encircled his head. As my identity was known at the Y. M. C. A., and as I was wearing my valuables, I did not dare reveal myself. But I was acutely lovesick the remainder of the day, pining to run across my friend again under circumstances such that I could greet him.

It actually chanced the following morning that I again encountered him, this time on the street several blocks distant from the Y. M. C. A.

Three where I was not recognized: I meet face to face a policeman on Broadway who was my very first companion at the opening of my life as a fairie ("Red Mike"). While secretary to a millionaire in the suburbs, I rode twelve miles in the same car with two Mulberry Street companions with whom I had passed many evenings. I would not allow them to see my face. A soldier with whom I, as Jennie June, became acquainted at a fort, came near, ten years previously, being a member of my Sunday school class. (I wish to remind the reader that I engaged in no religious work while yielding to the "procreative" instincts. I have always considered such a combination scandalous. Inverts, while committing no sin in following their instincts in moderation, should leave church work absolutely alone unless they are able to crucify their carnal desire.) I myself recognized the soldier only after learning his name, and that he came from my own native village. I of course did not let him know that we once attended the same church.

Two of my Stuyvesant Square friends once greeted me in a store, and another on a street car. In a large city several hundred miles from New York, I was greeted by an actor friend of my Fourteenth Street days. Three different times in cities several hundred miles from New York I was greeted by former soldiers with whom I had associated at forts in the suburbs of that city. A number of times in the heart of New York I ran across soldiers with whom I had associated at those forts. Once while in a theatre, a soldier a few seats back called out, "Jennie June," but I pretended not to hear him. On another occasion, while living in a small suburb, I was stopped near my home by a young man who asked if I could tell him "where a fellow they call 'Jennie June' lives?" Evidently he thought he recognized myself as Jennie June, but I boldly replied that I had never heard of such an individual. I feared a disclosure of my double life, but nothing eventuated.

While visiting my native village in 1907, where I was now a stranger to nearly all the inhabitants, one of a group of young men whom I passed called out: "Hello Jennie June! . . . Hello Jennie June! . . . Why don't you say something?" My appearing as if I did not hear him probably led him to conclude that he was mistaken. It is almost a miracle that the little community in which I was reared did not learn of my double life, since approximately four thousand young men knew me only as "Jennie June," about one-half of whom were at one time soldiers by profession, and therefore wanderers over the face of the earth.

In 1914, in New York City, almost in front of the building where I was employed, a Stuyvesant Square acquaintance of more than ten years before thought he recognized me, called out "Jennie June," and threw kisses. I pretended not to notice anything, which probably made him conclude he was mistaken.

Encounters with associates of my scholarly self while I was living out the life of "Jennie June" were almost equally numerous. While promenading the Bowery as a low-class fairie, I once passed a schoolmate from my native village, but he did not appear to recognize me. On two occasions while promenading Fourteenth Street as a high-class fairie, I passed university associates, but on only one occasion was there a sign of recognition. At neither time did my conduct happen to be suspicious.

While on a train returning from a frolic with soldiers of a fort in the suburbs, and somewhat disheveled, I rode in the same car with a university acquaintance, but avoided him, so that he probably did not recognize me. While entertaining at a shore resort a soldier to whom I was incognito, I ran across a near friend, to whom I was compelled to introduce the soldier. The friend was ever afterward cool and evidently suspected the truth. While walking with a ruffian of the slums, I was recognized by a chance travelling companion with whom I had sat at the same table for a week on a steamer. I denied my identity.

One evening when dressed rather shabbily and on a car bound for the slums, I was compelled to tip my hat to a lady friend who was also a passenger. I was thankful that it did not happen to be a male friend. When even in a more dilapidated condition, having spent the preceding night in the slums, and on a car bound for the room where I was to exchange my shabby clothes for my ordinary apparel, an intimate lady friend boarded the car. Hiding my face as best I could, I alighted at the next stop.

Once when my face had only just been battered up by violent blows, I rode several miles in the same car with a male acquaintance who possibly recognized me. While in bed in a hospital with my face all battered out of shape, I was under the care of a former physician, to whom however I never had had occasion to reveal that I was an invert. Though we had met a score of times intimately, he failed to recognize me on account of my extreme disfigurement, and I was ashamed to make myself known. I had of course registered at the hospital under an assumed name.

To return to the chance meeting on Broadway—I was face to face with the individual whom at the time I desired to meet above every one else in the world, but through fear of blackmail or other undesirable consequences, did not dare confess that I had ever seen. After a moment of speechlessness, and with voice trembling through fright, I answered, "You are mistaken in the person. I do not remember ever seeing you before."

"O you must remember me. You told me you were a waiter in a restaurant on the Bowery. Ain't you working there no more?"

"I never worked in a restaurant. You mistake me for some one else." Saying this I started to walk on.

"No, not just yet. I think I can convince you that we have met before." He mentions things that occurred at our former meetings. Although all that he said was true, I continued to refuse to admit my identity. Finally he lost patience: "Say, give me a dollar, will you? I haven't had anything to eat for two days. Hand it out, or I'll make it so hot for you right here that you'll wish you had!"

Expecting to be knocked into the gutter, or that something even worse was about to transpire, I yielded to his demand. He pocketed the money and went on his way. I saw slipping by perhaps the only opportunity of my life to make an appointment with the particular individual with whom at the time I was madly in love. I was also emboldened because I had found out that he would be easy with me. I ran after him and exclaimed: "I want to meet you again. Where do you hang out?"

"In Madison Square evenings."

I immediately turned down a side street and hid in a doorway in order to ascertain whether I was being followed. From that meeting I rejoiced in the hope of future intimacy with one of my favorites of the Bowery period, and on the three following evenings wearily promenaded Madison Square for hours in search of him. On the third evening I with great joy discovered him seated alone. Eagerly approaching, I aped, as usual on such occasions, the voice and manners of a baby girl, while I began a graceful dance with various muscles of my body, motions occasionally aroused under sexual excitement. For the first time in nearly six months I adopted the rôle of "Jennie June," and it gave me great satisfaction.

"My beautiful, beautiful Jew boy, I feared I would never see you again. Say, do you know you are beautiful? Do you know you are beautiful?"

"What do you do now since you don't work in a restaurant?"

"I . . . I," I stammered, caught unawares, and seeking to invent something in order to hide my true station in life. "I now work in a shoe-store over on 3rd Avenue."

"I suppose you intend doing the right thing by me tonight. I am in hard luck. I just had three dollars stolen off me."

After a few minutes' conversation, we proceeded westward along 26th Street, bound for the dark and at night deserted quarter known as Hell's Kitchen, along the margin of the Hudson River. It is perhaps the most dangerous part of New York at night, but here we could be absolutely alone. Most of the district is covered with lumber yards, freight terminals, etc., and the very few persons who frequent those streets at night are likely to be ruffians and dockrats of the most vicious character.

Arrived within half a block of the Hudson River, we seated ourselves on the platform of a storehouse, and I began to kiss passionately my companion's face, hair, and hands, and even covered his clothing with kisses. While thus engaged, only one person passed, a man, apparently intoxicated, staggering along in the direction of the river and on the opposite side of the street. He did not appear to notice us and was soon lost in the darkness toward the river, whereupon my uneasiness in large part passed away. On such occasions as this—on the public street—I always had a mortal fear of being surprised and beaten to death, prejudice against androgynes being so great.

After the "intoxicated" man had passed out of sight, we were undisturbed for five minutes. During this interval, my companion gave a low whistle several times, which made me nervous and suspicious, and I delayed incriminating myself. Always, too, I liked to spoon a long time with my companion as a preliminary. If I had been with any one else, such whistling would have made me take to my heels, but my present companion was not a perfect stranger, and on our previous meetings had done me no harm. As I feared, the young Jew's whistling turned out to be his means of communication with a confederate, the man who had passed feigning intoxication. When I had met the young Jew in the Square, a confederate was watching a short distance away, and he had followed us into Hell's Kitchen. As I had been the victim of assault and robbery so many times, usually when walking off to a lonely place with a companion, I took care that we were not followed by any of his pals. But as my present companion seemed like an old acquaintance, I did not take my usual precautions.

As eavesdropper, it was desirable to approach from the west, since a high fence prevented a good view from the east, and an approach from that direction would have immediately aroused my suspicions that he was a confederate. He had therefore adopted the ruse of intoxication in order to get to the west of us. While I was engaged in my adoration, the form of a powerfully built man about twenty-eight years of age silently and suddenly emerged out of the obscurity in the direction of the river. Always alert on such occasions on the public street, I perceived him sooner than he intended. He no doubt intended to surprise me in an incriminating position. At the moment of my discovery, my companion sought by main force to hold me in a humiliating position, but I struggled and prevented it. On seeing that his original plan was frustrated through my alertness, the eavesdropper came forward, passed himself off as the watchman of the store-house, and sternly demanded of me what business we had there.

"Only sitting down and resting," I replied all in a tremble.

"This is a queer place to sit down and rest in. Tell me what yous two was doin' here, or I'll have you locked up."

"We were only talking together."

"Only talkin' together? What did yous walk a mile from Madison Square fur?" On hearing this question, I first realized that the man was a confederate. I replied that we were just out for a walk.

"Do you ginerally take walks to a lonesome place as this where there's nothin' to see?" Then he addressed my companion, "How long you known this feller?"

"I met him tonight in Madison Square for the first."

"People don't ginerally take walks together to such places as this when they just happen to meet in parks! Out wid it, what was this feller doin' wid you?"

On my companion accusing me of fellatio, the man feigned surprise and abhorrence, and started to grab me. But I nimbly sprang away, and fairly flew eastward, with them at my heels. After sprinting an eighth of a mile, I felt my speed decreasing. It seemed as if I scarcely moved at all. My legs trembled under me, my breath came and went in sonorous gasps, and my heart beat audibly. I could hear the footfalls of my pursuers, now gaining upon me. As I ran I constantly besought Providence that they might stumble and fall, or give up the chase as hopeless.

Arrived within a hundred feet of 10th Avenue, I felt all my powers failing, and at every step expected to fall to the ground, perhaps dead, as I had some valvular disease of the heart. If I fell westward of 10th Avenue, where there would be no possibility of witnesses, I feared the ruffians would beat me to death in their anger at my causing them this hard chase. I hoped to hold out until I could throw myself on the mercy of pedestrians whom I expected to encounter on 10th Avenue, a street lined with a poor class of tenement houses. I reached that avenue and ran north half a block until I overtook a company of four smartly dressed young men. I now stopped running, walked along directly in front of them, and believed my pursuers would withdraw. But the latter seized me violently, and I appealed to the four spectators: "Won't you please keep these fellows from touching me? They are thieves, and were trying to beat and rob me."

"What's the matter? What's the matter?"

"Wait till I kin git my breath and I'll tell you."

"They are thieves and I was running away from them. They are blackmailers, that's all they are. A few days ago on Broadway they got some money out of me, and now are trying it again."

"He is a c——. I found him down on 26th Street wid this young feller."

"I didn't do anything of the kind to him. They are just trying to blackmail me."

"All they want is money. Just hand out four or five dollars and they'll let you alone. It is worth that to you to get out of this scrape."

"But I haven't done anything why I should pay them money, and I haven't that much money with me."

"You've admitted they are blackmailing you, so you must have done something pretty bad. We will leave you in their hands to take you to the police station. You ought to be locked up and have this cannibalism of yourn taken out of you."

"Please do me the favor not to leave me alone with them. They will kill me on the way. Please go along to the police station."

They all agreed to do so. But the more I saw of the character of the four smartly dressed young men, who were between twenty and twenty-five years of age, the more did I fear them, and I hoped we might encounter a policeman, so that I might voluntarily surrender myself to the toils of the law, as I expected to be killed by this party. But I have learned by experience that a policeman can never be found when needed most. Some civilian pedestrians were met, but I was afraid of the consequences of appealing to them.

Arrived at 29th Street, they stated their purpose of leading me down this particularly dark and deserted thoroughfare, probably in order to assault and rob me, and this prospect made me more anxious than ever to be delivered out of their hands. A chance of deliverance presented itself. There are steam railroad tracks in the middle of 10th Avenue and a long freight train happened to be passing slowly. Two horse-cars, each containing several passengers, were waiting at the corner of 29th Street until the train passed. The four drivers and conductors were all outside. As my captors led me within three feet of one of the platforms, I suddenly broke away and attempted to board the car. But they jerked me away, struggling and crying out to the conductor, only an arm's length distant: "I want to board this car and they won't let me! Won't you please make them leave me alone?"

But he did not make a move or say a word, any more than if he had been a statue. The other three drivers and conductors were likewise interested spectators, but made no move to help me. When I saw their inaction, I screamed "Help! Help!" hoping to alarm the passengers. Such a procedure angered my captors to the exploding point, and they all pitched into me, threw me to the ground, pounded me, kicked me, and stamped upon me. The two conductors stood for a moment directly over my prostrate body, but remained neutral. I screamed as I have never screamed on any other occasion, but none of the passengers appeared to hear me.

In about a minute the train had passed and the two horse-cars started on their way. As I saw them disappearing and leaving me alone with my assailants, all hope of life departed. I found myself exceedingly calm and resigned to my fate. My life and consciousness seemed to be flickering, ready to be entirely extinguished. The next thing I knew, I was vomiting violently, and then my senses began to come back. I found myself all alone, and also found that my pockets had been ransacked.

For several days my whole body was so sore as to make it painful to move about. Moreover, for several days I experienced a season of mental depression with impulses toward suicide. Few souls ever had such a burden to bear. Yet the world has no sympathy for these unhappiest of mortals, the refined sexual inverts. Thousands of them are driven to suicide out of every generation, and yet the world is unmoved by their sorrows. Every other human creature when in sorrow and trouble receives comfort from his fellows, but mankind heaps sorrow on sorrow upon the head of the already despairing invert. Even his own family turn their backs on him and disown him.

About this time, thoughts came to me of going over to London or Paris, far from my family, where they could never learn of my shame, and passing the remainder of my youth wholly given up to the life of a fille de joie. But I did not take this step, chiefly out of love for my parents, to save them sorrow on my account.

I have now reached a period of my life lasting over two years during which it was my luck to serve as private secretary to a millionaire septuagenarian living in the suburbs of the metropolis. Though surrounded with all the comforts of wealth, and having every opportunity for intellectual growth and enjoyment, the "procreative" instinct allowed me no rest. At times I would wish for a life of poverty in the slums with a mate to living in my refined and elegant surroundings without any opportunity for gratification of this instinct. I found it absolutely necessary to spend one night out of fourteen in the city's slums. The curative value of a good environment is evident from the fact that I was fully satisfied with that frequency.

The *Why* of a double life has already been sufficiently indicated—namely, at least in my own case, mental peculiarity, a constitution different from the normal. Does the reader suppose the author led a double life because he *wanted* to? Not at all, but simply because Nature and society forced it upon him. Many could remain celibate all their days with no sense of a great void in their life, and with no suffering to themselves; but the author, remaining celibate much beyond a month, would ordinarily rave, as a drug-victim raves when unable to obtain his anodyne. It is a confession that I shrink from making, but I feel that medical science should know it. At this period of my life I had to escape to the slums to find opportunity for fellatio in order to save myself from fellatio cum cani magno. The involuntary desire for fellatio was irresistible and I would have sacrificed everything for it. I trust all my readers are broadminded enough to see that I was irresponsible for this condition, and that it was entirely counter to my own wishes.

Secondly, the author was not at all to be blamed for having recourse to the slums. For me it was the only way then open to satisfy the most exacting demands of Nature. To frequent the forts had not yet been seriously considered. How easy it is, comparatively, for the normal man to gratify the procreative instinct! The man of high moral ideals can in most cases marry, and possess his beloved every day and night, not for only a few hours each month, as was the case with me during nearly all my career. The rake obtains all the companions he wishes with no risk of suffering violence. But an androgyne, if having any regard for his reputation, has often, as already seen, to run the gauntlet of assault, robbery, imprisonment, and even death, when he seeks his counterpart. To no respectable young man of my acquaintance did I dare make known my dreadful secret, which I believed would alienate from me every respectable member of society who should learn it. Because of society's misunderstanding and prejudging my peculiarity, I was compelled to run the risks of the slums. Mankind would ostracize me for it, but instead they should pity me as one with whom the Almighty has dealt very bitterly.

Some eminent men in all callings are numbered among the inverts. Their terrible secret is hidden from the world. If it should become known, they are irretrievably lost, and would be ostracized with the greatest possible disgust and repugnance, although these emotions have no basis in reason. These inverts, who were brought up in refinement and hold honorable positions in society, deplore their lot in life. They greatly regret that they have to resort to such shameful and lamentable means as they do. By reason of the universal hatred of mankind for those of the race who are built on a different plan from the vast majority, these inverts, well educated, holding an honorable position in the world, and possessing a good income, are necessarily driven to subterfuges, artifices, and deceptions of which the world, which now holds them in honor, would believe them incapable. But they suffer from a craving which *must* be satisfied, even at the risk of the loss of property, reputation, life itself. This craving, which medical writers like Krafft-Ebing, who have made a study of the phenomenon, say is, in its intensity, often immeasurably beyond the normal procreative instinct in man, drives these unfortunates to "pick up" a poor young man whom they come across in a part of the city remote from where they are known. But everywhere there are traps set for these unfortunates—truly unfortunates, since their repulsive instincts are no fault of their own, being congenital—and in their search for the mate which is necessary for their contented existence, they sometimes come to grief. Not only does the blackmailer spread his net for these stepchildren of nature. The civil authorities have also their detectives out after them.

The *How* of a double life during this period of my career will now be described. On the eve of one of my fortnightly female-impersonation sprees, the reader probably supposes that I would be happy in anticipation. On the contrary, a great weight of sorrow and anxiety always oppressed me. There was of course an attraction which drew me to the city, but it was more than counterbalanced by the realization of the risks of my losing my then enviable position in life, and the dread of the danger I had to put myself in, in order to obtain the satisfaction of my instincts. A peculiar phenomenon was vivid images of violent blows in the face, since I had been the victim of such a number of times. But even apart from the dread of the real dangers, even if there were no such dangers, an overwhelming feeling of sadness and anxiety always came over me as the time to go forth on my peculiar quest approached. On the eve of a female-impersonation spree during this period, I always felt like a soldier on entering a great battle from which he realized he might never come back alive, or like a murderer on the eve of his electrocution. On such occasions I habitually sang to myself:

> *"Why oh why should we be melancholy, boys,*
> *Whose business 'tis to die?"*

Just before leaving my residence, I always knelt and prayed the Heavenly Father to bring me back safe, and on my return likewise my first act was to thank Him for it. Arrived in New York, my melancholy and dread would almost entirely disappear, and in their place a sense of gladness would spring up that in the great metropolis I was lost to all who knew me. I was in the habit of putting up at a third-class hotel in a poor quarter of the city, registering under an assumed name. About eight in the evening, I would retire to my room, remove my outer clothing, conceal my valuables, dress myself in a rather shabby suit, and saunter forth, hurrying past hotel employees so that they would not observe my change of apparel. Reaching the Bowery or some other street among those named in the account of my "low-class fairie" period, I would experience a feeling of exultation at finding myself again on Jennie June's stamping ground. I had left behind all my masculinity, such as it was. The feminine in me, suppressed for two weeks, now held sway. My first care was to hide a reserve fund in a small black box on a ledge of the old market on the site of the present Police Headquarters on Centre Street.

I occasionally visited the scene of my fairie apprenticeship on Mulberry Street. But a resident adolescent once remarked with much truth: "You come around here looking like a tramp, but we have seen you up on Fifth Avenue with fine clothes on. You look as though you didn't have a cent, but your shoes are full of money." For success with this class, it is almost necessary that an invert be looked upon as belonging to the same social stratum.

On one occasion I was turned over to a policeman by a blackmailer, but the former refused to arrest me, although he believed the accusations.

On another evening when I had not come to the city for a female-impersonation spree, but nevertheless took a walk on the Bowery, I scraped acquaintance with a high-class adolescent from the country who was stranded in the city. We walked down a side street until we came to a deserted block, and entered the pitch-dark portal of a closed factory. But a huckster on the nearest corner happened to notice us skulk into the portal, and supposing we were thieves, notified the first policeman who passed, who sought another policeman that they might together investigate. The two suddenly confronted us. I was horror-struck, as it was the worst possible time for me to be arrested since I had on me marks of my identity. They searched us and then made a correct guess. One said with reference to me: "This fellow is a ———. We won't touch him because he can't help it, but we'll give this other fellow a good clubbing." They made us depart in opposite directions, clubbing my companion a little.

On another evening I had been robbed of all my money. When we reached the street I demanded back part of it. But my companion shouted "Police! Police!" in order to frighten me away, saying he was going to have me arrested because I was an invert. To a couple of young men he cried out: "This fellow is a ———. Call a cop for me, will you? I want to have him arrested." But those addressed were too busy to interfere. A horse-car then happened along, on which he jumped. I ran behind for a hundred feet, crying to the conductor on the rear platform: "Put him off! He's a thief! He has robbed me!" But neither the conductor nor the men passengers on the platform cared to interfere.

I occupied a room with a young ruffian at a third-class hotel other than that where I had left my ordinary clothing and valuables. Before retiring I withdrew to the toilet-room and placed the bulk of my money, a five-dollar bill, in the toe of a sock. As I undressed, I was careful to throw it far under the bed. After half an hour, we closed our eyes. But I intended to remain awake until he had fallen asleep in order to hide the door key lest he leave with my money and clothing while I slept. He intended to remain awake until I slept, and then depart as described. He tried to soothe me to sleep, exactly like a mother her infant, but finally losing all hope, said: "Do you know how much you can get for this? Twenty years in state's prison!"

He dressed, ransacked my clothing, and then tied it in a bundle to carry away, repeatedly warning me not to interfere under penalty of arrest. I lay in consternation, meditating what steps to take. He finally

A steamboat flirtation: In my extensive globe-trotting, only two or three times did I indulge in coquetry on a public conveyance, for fear of disgrace or even robbery. But on the present occasion I was so smitten that I took the risk. I had occasion to accompany my employer on a trip to Boston. We went by the all-sea route around Cape Cod. During the evening my employer preferred to remain inside, while I was out on deck. I discovered a handsome adolescent seated alone, clad in a golf suit, which always heightened to me a young man's charms. I seated myself near him, dying with desire to enter into conversation, but for a while unable to surmount my bashfulness. But I soon began a conversation which lasted a large part of the night. I drew from him the whole story of his life. His last adventure had been a bicycle ride from Boston to New York. The more I gazed at him, the more I heard about his life, and the more I read his character from his countenance, his manners, and his adventures, the more did I discover in him lovable qualities. His ravishing beauty, his countenance ever beaming with smiles, his kindly disposition toward me, his hot sensual nature, his fearlessness, dare-deviltry, and thorough recklessness, and his intense masculinity in general, attracted me so strongly that I became ready—as already stated—to run the great risk of disclosing to my employer my perverted nature, and thus losing the excellent position I held. We talked on numerous subjects. After I had ascertained that he was a good-hearted fellow who would not easily take offense, and a Don Juan, I began to prepare to disclose my nature.

"You have a beautiful golf suit on."

"I shall never wear the rag again except to go skating in next winter."

"You must not do that. It sets your form off beautifully. You are the handsomest and the best-dressed fellow on the boat."

"Thank you. I'd give you a quarter for the compliment if I had the change."

"You appear to think I am flattering you, or making sport of you, but I mean what I say. You have a beautiful build, and know how to dress in good taste."

"From my hips down I am well enough built, but higher up I am too skinny."

"Not a bit of it. You are just perfection all over. Your form is as beautiful as that of Apollo."

After a while, before I had been able to come to the point of distinctly disclosing that I was an invert, he said he must go inside on account of the chilliness of the air, and I plead with him not to go.

"I'll see you later."

"Be sure not to forget. I shall be in misery until you are again by my side."

He laughed, apparently not yet fully understanding my feeling for him, and departed. A moment later I myself went inside, and took a seat beside my employer. My new acquaintance happened to pass, and gave me the sweetest, most loving smile I ever received. I was dying to follow the smiler, but feared my employer would detect my attraction. After several minutes, I followed in the direction in which he had disappeared, and finding him seated alone a little distance off, I whispered: "Come out on deck."

We seated ourselves close together. It was dark and there were no others sitting very near. I took one of his hands in mine, and asked if I might kiss it. He replied: "You can do anything to me you want to."

I now opened my heart to him fully. Though I loved him even to frenzy, I found him hardly less drawn to me. He reciprocated my affection as no lover ever before. We sat together for hours. Soon all the other passengers had retired, and I reclined in my lord's arms. Long after midnight, my lord, desiring to get some sleep, repeatedly requested me to leave him for the night, saying we could meet again in Boston. But I knew that on account of my being in the company of my employer, I could never meet the young man again, and could not yet tear myself away. Several times he good-humoredly wrenched himself from my grip, saying he must get some sleep. But each time, advancing toward the taff-rail, I would call out: "I am going to jump into the sea if you leave me alone." With other intimates, I had used the ruse of suicide if they did not yield to my entreaties, but they had only replied: "If you want to be such a fool as to kill yourself, I won't stop you." But this noble fellow ran after me and restrained me, and said he would sit up a little longer.

Towards four A.M., the poor young man was in a predicament as to how to get rid of me, who had lost my reason. He was of such a kindly disposition that he did not wish to hurt or offend me, but my continuous kisses and caresses finally became so annoying that in the hope of bringing an end to them, not at all with malice, he clutched me by the throat as if in anger. But I exclaimed: "Your cruelty only makes me love you the more!" and again started in to cover him with kisses— hair, face, hands, arms, and clothing, even his shoes.

"You must want to get into your mouth all the dust I picked up off the road yesterday."

"That's just what I do. Its coming into contact with your dear body has transformed it and etherialized it. Oh, I love you so much! So much! No other girl ever worshipped her lord as I worship you. I know it is wrong to hate, and I pray God to forgive me, but I now feel only hatred toward everybody who stands in the way of our being one, and living out our lives together."

After some time, as a last resort, pretending to be very angry, he kicked me, and ordered me to go down to the other end of the boat. Such treatment humiliated and saddened me, because I thought it an evidence that I was despised. I immediately became repentant for having so imposed on his good nature, asked his pardon, and departed.

When I left, I expected never to set eyes on him again. The next morning I purposely lay abed very late, in order that he might have taken his departure before I should leave my state-room. I was afraid he might encounter me with my employer, and in some way betray to the latter my sexual peculiarity. But as it happened, he also did not leave the boat until late, and caught sight of me seated at the breakfast table with my employer. On seeing him approach, I was stricken with terror, fearing he might denounce me. As he passed, I hardly dared look at him. He made a sign for me to rise and follow him. For fear my employer might somehow suspect something, and in order to discourage any farther approach, I appeared not to notice his beckoning. Moreover, I did not dare follow him immediately, though I would have given a fortune to have been at full liberty to do so. I realized that I might be losing forever a companion and mate for life whom I slavishly adored.

Five minutes afterward, as soon as I felt I could leave my employer's side without exciting his suspicion, I followed in the direction the young man had taken, but saw nothing of him. Wringing my hands in desperation, I rushed all over the vessel, peering into every nook and corner. Then I went out on the wharf, and looked everywhere there. I returned on board, and searched the whole boat from top to bottom three times before giving up in despair. What a pang went through my heart when I found he had gone and I not heard the message he had evidently wished to give me! Never before in my life had I regretted anything as much as not having inquired his name and address. As I was unwilling to give my own, I did not like to ask for his. Furthermore, during our evening together, I did not anticipate we could ever meet again, and so thought it useless to ask. He, probably, as well as I, preferred that his identity remain unknown.

I had rarely felt more disconsolate, or more angry with the world, and I experienced but little pleasure during my week in Boston. All the time, the thought uppermost in my mind was to run across this young man again. I spent as much time as possible in the most frequented localities, peering into the face of every young man who passed to see if he were not the one for whom I was pining. Several nights, after my employer had retired, I stole out of my room, and seated myself on the steps of the most frequented subway station until midnight, in the forlorn hope of meeting by chance one particular individual out of the million in the Boston metropolitan district.

He had informed me that he was an electrician. I spent many hours in calling at shops where such workmen had their headquarters. Under some pretext, I obtained permission to go through the works, and looked over every young man employed there. I wrote letters to a number of his trade whose names I found in the city directory, inquiring whether I had met them on the steamer. On returning to New York, I engaged an electrical apprentice to continue the search, but all my efforts proved fruitless.

I now spent five months in Europe with my employer. I was generally free evenings, and during our stay in the large cities, spent two or three a week with beaux that I came across. I had considerable conversational ability in four foreign languages. In Paris I generally spent my evenings with the adolescent porters of the Gare St. Lazaire, and in Berlin with soldiers whom I met in the Tiergarten. Because of indiscretions, I came near being arrested in Berlin and in Naples. In only one instance in Europe was an attempt made to extort money from me, and I yielded rather than get into trouble.

My flirtations in Europe were uneventful. I had to be far more cautious there for fear of getting into trouble, and associate with my beaux clad as a prosperous citizen. As they necessarily knew that I was a person of attainments much higher than the average, I was restrained from going far in impersonation of a young woman or a baby. I found that throughout the large cities, fairies were as well known to the ultra-virile adolescents as in New York, and the latter were equally susceptible to the advances of the former.

In my unusually wide travels in America, I have never been accosted by a pervert or an invert. But during my five months' sojourn in Europe, I was one evening accosted in one of the great capitals by a fairie sixteen years of age, and in another I was accosted in a park by an urning of twenty-six (that is, a man who craved mutual onanism). My impression is that the inhabitants of the large cities of Europe are more sex-mad than those of American cities of similar size. In one of the great capitals (which I do not name out of charity) inversion and perversion were frightful—incomparably more open, at least, than in New York. It was my impression that there is more evanescent homosexuality—due to lack of opportunities with the opposite sex—than in America. Apparently the denser the population, the more widely extended is homosexuality.

In 1899 I was attracted by the German and the Dutch soldiers, but incomparably less than by the American soldier. They did not appear to be as powerfully built or as handsome, nor as wild and reckless. Their uniforms impressed me as far less fascinating. I was not at all attracted by the French soldiers, because I did not like their uniform, particularly the red baggy trousers, and because facial hirsute appendages are decidedly abhorrent to me. Likewise the British, Swiss, and Italian uniforms impressed me as detracting from the masculinity of the wearer instead of powerfully contributing to it, as the American uniform. The

German, Dutch, and particularly the American soldiers were the only ones that came up to my idea of demigods.

On a sojourn in the Old World in 1911, I found myself admiring the Moroccan, Spanish, Portuguese, and Russian soldiers to about the same degree as I have always admired the American. Indeed the Russians impressed me as the most bewitching in the world, because they are the most gigantic and the most savage-looking. I now came also to find the British and the Italian uniforms rather attractive, but liked the French and Swiss no better than before. In this later lengthy sojourn, I did not once seek a beau, and had only feeble desires to do so, whereas twelve years before I had a fierce, irresistible, obsession to be with them as much as possible. But most of all, I was restrained by the presence of my employer, who left me no good opportunity to seek other company.

After holding my position as private secretary during my middle twenties for over two years, I was compelled to resign because a tradesman's driver who frequently delivered goods at the house of my employer chanced to identify me while two ruffians were demanding blackmail on the Bowery. I was denounced to the truckdriver as a ——. Several years afterward I learned that knowledge of the incident probably never reached my employer.

At this point in my life I wrote the present autobiography down to the year arrived at (1899), having previously kept copious diaries.

The scene of the last six years of my open career as a fairie, still to be described, lay in the neighborhood of—and in large part on—the military reservations in the suburbs. Providence granted me the fulfillment of a fond dream of years before—to be a soldiers' mignon. I now decided to devote exclusively to young Mars the remainder of my youth—for with me the period of youth continued abnormally long, at least until my early thirties. In 1899, at the age of twenty-five, I successfully, as Jennie June, passed for twenty. At the close of my open career, when I was thirty-one, I passed for twenty-four. As already remarked, business associates who have not had the least suspicion of my being an invert—chiefly because they did not know of the existence of such people—have declared even down to my middle forties that I have not ceased to be remarkably childlike both physically and psychically. If I had had the physique and psychical constitution of the ordinary man, the career I am outlining would have been impossible. But Nature has given the fairie a physique and mentality *sui generis.*

For a passive invert to make captives of ultra-virile adolescents, he must be youthful, with facial hair eradicated or clean-shaven, of somewhat feminine physique, looks, and manners, a good female-impersonator, and an expert coquette. Many inverts lack these qualities that are necessary to insure a successful career as a fairie, and the vast majority have no desires along this line. Some inverts, as well as some females, seem to be predestined by Nature for the profession of fille de joie.

On the other hand, the professional fairie of the lowest class of public house could not have had the long career around the forts that I had because the soldiers would not have tolerated the presence there of such a depraved being. The second half of my open career was possible because while having the coquetry and craze for venery of the depraved fairie, I had also the refinement, outward modesty, and general rectitude which are to be expected in an androgyne brought up as a puritan and graduated at a university. I repeat that throughout my career as a fairie—apart from the coquetry and venery just named—I lived up to the highest ethical standards, and never knowingly inflicted the least detriment on a single soul.

More than once before the opening of this second half of my open career, I had thought that my period of flirtation was at an end. Particularly on account of my age, having now entered my twenty-sixth year, I had thought no more romantic adventures could be mine. But it turned out that these six years, even the last of them, when I was thirty-one, were full of adventures as romantic as I had ever had.

When I dedicated myself to the career of a soldiers' mignon, I was well aware that these men are particularly subject to venereal disease—and I ultimately contracted anal and buccal venereal warts, syphilis, and gonorrhea from them, whereas during the first half of my career, I had had close to 700 liaisons with civilian adolescents without contracting any disease so far as I knew. But I gladly assumed this greatly increased risk because of the ultravirility and general terribleness of the class in question. This terribleness is applicable only to the professional common soldier when the nation is at peace.

I asked an unusually attractive artilleryman whom I met on the Bowery if I might visit him at his barracks, and one evening made the journey. I was conducted to his squad-room, but he was not in. I found myself in what was to me a sensual paradise containing about a dozen youthful soldiers busy at different things. I could not think of departing even though my friend was out. I began to talk effeminately and babyishly. I was immediately hailed as a fairie, and shown to a seat on a bunk, having around me the arms of two soldiers, with several others sitting or lying on the same bunk and caressing me. It was almost the same as if a maiden had suddenly appeared in their midst. I outwomaned woman for their entertainment and because I was fascinated.

I was so enthusiastically received that I made the decision already described, and for the period of a little more than two years visited this military reservation one evening a week, devoting all the rest of my time to scholarly pursuits.

For some weeks I enjoyed the rare pleasure of association with my idols in a squad-room or in a non-commissioned officer's private room, and had the run of all the other rooms, since practically everybody looked upon me the same as on an unoffending tabby-cat that might invade their quarters. I was even put to bed in the barracks as tenderly as a mother puts her babe in its cradle.

I have always shrunk with horror from handling the weapons of warfare myself, but they had a wonderful fascination for me when in the hands of soldiers, or when seen stacked in the squad-rooms.

A typical evening in a squad-room: On my entering, the soldiers shout goodnaturedly: "Hello Jennie, old girl!"

"Hello all you big braves!"

The rumor soon spreads to other squad-rooms that "Jennie June" is making a visit, and a score or more soon gather about me. I always came loaded down with cigarettes and other things that soldiers are fond of, except intoxicants. One youthful soldier after another rolls back his sleeves and displays tattooed figures for me to rave over: "That proves you are completely masculine, and I worship you for having it done." Others double back their right arms and let me feel of their biceps: "I call you 'Strength!' I call you 'Power!' I call you a man of iron! Mighty man of war! Mighty man of valor! Mighty man of renown!"

Later one who meets me for the first time asks: "Do you call yourself a girl? In all my life I never vidi puellam cum peni!"

"I know I am only part girl. I have a girl's mind and breasts and my body otherwise is much like a girl's."

"If you don't believe Jennie is a girl, just feel of her breasts."

Several stick their hands into my bosom. "He's got a girl's breasts all right."

They ask me to sing, listen attentively, and then remark: "That is a high tenor. It has an effect on the voice all right."

"Are you and I of the same sex?" I ask, taking pleasure in our physical and psychical contrasts.

"No, Jennie, you are a baby, and we are the big, big braves."

My presence would inspire them to an evening of innocent frolicking, and they would play pranks on me, for example, dancing around the room shrieking like wild Indians, brandishing their swords, and banging them on the floor. I would respond to their pranks in the manner they were looking for. They thought that I had only the mental capacity of a girl-boy weakling, as I did not compose my own songs until after more than two years of association with them.

In the barracks I was always outwardly modest and frowned on decidedly improper advances, but my venery in private soon set a minority against me so that entrance to the barracks was forbidden.

I had a craze for hecatontandry, and achieved it. In a letter I wrote: "You know by that act (fellatio), you and I are bound together in a new and close relation of friendship, in a sort of wedlock. We stand henceforth forever in the relation of husband and wife, whether you will or not. Therefore please always remember me as more nearly related to you, more completely a part of your life and being, than your soldier comrades."

In summer I would linger after retreat near the gate of the fort to watch the soldiers start out to seek their evening's recreation. A hundred would pass, and nearly every one call out a pleasant greeting: "Hello sweetheart!" "Hello little wife!" I would reply: "Hello you dare-devil!" "Hello you dark-eyed beauty!" etc.

I was occasionally robbed or blackmailed by evilminded ones, and was several times handed over to the police by such as misunderstood me. But the police always refused to place me under arrest, and even acted as a bodyguard against the very few soldiers who loathed an effeminate male and sought to inflict pain. My conduct in public was always above reproach, although I have been forced at night on a public road by half-intoxicated adolescents who happened to run across me. Discovery in the bushes by pedestrians only thirty feet away would have placed me in peril of long imprisonment. On one occasion the two soldiers had threatened to cut my throat if I made a sound, and they themselves did not stir from their positions (Simul fellatio atque paedicatio).

As to the ethics of my conduct in the vicinity of the barracks, it was not immoral. The ordinary woman has only one lord, to whom she is bound "until death do part." My lot was to have practically at one time a hundred, who were not forcibly and permanently linked up with me. There were not the reasons for monandry and for permanency that exist in the former case. As to race-suicide, my associates were legally bound not to rear families. From the standpoint of their health, relations with me were safer than with the ordinary purveyors. Furthermore, they told me that no exhaustion supervened the next day, as in my own case. I was not bent primarily on coition, but on social intercourse tinged with flirtation. I never solicited. It was not necessary, as every one knew me.

Over two years now went by of an existence rendered very delectable by reason of association with young Mars one evening a week, all the rest of my time, as usual, being devoted to scholarly pursuits. I was then called upon to say good-by—as I feared—forever—to my much coveted position of pet of a fort, which I was in large measure. Spermatorrhea, from which I had suffered acutely since the age of sixteen, had come to a crisis. For the past two years, while looking to be in good health, I had suffered intensely from mental and physical prostration, due almost entirely to exclamations during sleep but in small part to nervous shock following fellatio.

Neurasthenia now confined me for six months to the village home of my parents. The "procreative" instinct gave me no rest, just as a drug fiend has none when denied his anodyne. Night after night I roamed the streets in the factory section. On two occasions I was successful. On a third I was crazed by enforced abstinence for over a month. I encountered a youth just under puberty. I clandestinely ascertained that he did not know me, did not attend the same church, and was employed in a part of the village where he was not likely to run across me. I was a shoemaker, just arrived in the village looking for work. I was lonely and languishing for company. A burden was oppressing me and I needed a confidant. Would he be my confidant? Would he promise to keep strictly to himself what I was about to tell? Had he heard of hermaphrodites?[3] I was one.

I found that to permit fellatio was decidedly against his tastes, and plead earnestly that he would show me compassion, at the same time offering money. His final answer was: "I was not brought up that way. I would never permit it. I am a Christian."

Fearing he would raise an alarm, and I would be arrested and my family disgraced, I sprinted away. After a few seconds I looked back to see whether I was followed. My terror produced the hallucination of a mob. I sprinted around corner after corner and did not rest until some distance outside the village, where I found a hiding place and moaned and complained to my Creator over my lot.

I was now afraid to show myself in the village, and unutterably downcast at being the victim of an obsession which led me to commit what are commonly regarded as revolting crimes. From this consideration, and also because of the wrecking of my health through emissions during sleep, I decided on immediate castration. Minor motives were that I would prefer to possess one less mark of the male, and that I thought the facial hair cells would cease to function and I thus be rid of my most detested and most troublesome badge of masculinity.

---

3. As this term is commonly a part of the vocabulary of laboring men, I sometimes used it in reference to myself, as they would not have understood the proper term. I am of course not an hermaphrodite in the present signification of that term.

From the age of seventeen to nineteen, on the day following an exclamation during sleep, I would be feeble, very forgetful, and would stammer. From nineteen on, after I had begun to yield to instinct, the ill effects were much less marked until during my twenty-eighth year—the point of time at which this autobiography has arrived—when my eyes were dim for one or two days following, my hearing was somewhat disarranged, and my heart abnormal in its action. During this period of eleven years, various remedies prescribed by physicians were without effect. I happened to be a globe-trotter, and thereby discovered that travelling, particularly sea voyages, much diminished the exclamations. It is necessary here to remind the reader that both solitary and mutual onanism were always entirely unknown to me, and that in my sexual life, my pudenda were practically non-existent.

Castration, by removing the exhausting effects of emissions, gave me a new lease on life. I also believe it saved to me my sight and hearing. But with the testicles I lost a very large part of my physical strength. I was a semi-invalid for five years following. For example, the upper limit of my afternoon walks declined from ten to three miles. But my debility did not affect my looks or interfere seriously with the practice of my profession. If, on days when I felt tolerably vigorous, I stirred about uncommonly, I would be prostrated for from two to seven days following. It appeared as if the muscular waste was not eliminated from the blood as before castration, but remained in my system as a poison, rendering me dazed, taking the edge off my intellect, and enervating my body. I could spare my mental faculties for use in my profession only by leading a very quiet life, slow and limited in physical movement.

But beginning about five years after castration and continuing for ten years, I was physically as vigorous as before. Apparently my system found some other way of accomplishing the alteration in the blood usually the work of the testicles. Simultaneously with this return of my strength, the increase in adipose tissue following castration in large part disappeared. For ten years I remained in this physical condition, when suddenly, within about six weeks, adipose tissue rapidly increased and has rendered my figure for two years, down to the date of writing (1918), that "of a fat frau in the last stages of pregnancy," to quote the words of business associates. I simultaneously returned to the low degree of physical strength obtaining immediately after castration.

The following is my weight, stripped, at various ages; 20–25, 110 pounds; at castration at 27, 128; 29–32, 143; 32–42, 133; two years following (1916–1918), 160. After castration it required two years to rise gradually from 128 to 143. My obesity is entirely due to castration, as slenderness is universal in my family.

After castration, exclamations during sleep gradually declined in frequency, but continued, with the emission of a sticky fluid of the appearance of semen, for about nine months. But dreams of exclamations—that is, a sort of pseudo-exclamations—occurred about once a fortnight for several years, and about once in three months as late as fourteen years after castration. I would be dreaming of fellatio, and seemed to feel the muscular contractions that take place during exclamation. Awakening in alarm, it seemed that I must find some fluid, but did not.

Even up to more than three years after castration, I occasionally during fellatio experienced the spasm, when I could distinctly feel the contractions ductus ejaculatorii, as if to push along the semen, although nothing would exude. At those times I would utter a spasmodic groan.

Fourteen years after castration, when I had not experienced an emission for six years, I was with a companion who held the palm for amativeness among all that I had known. Amplexus ejus fervidi induxerunt in me emissionem copiosam. I immediately dismissed him because of my extreme exhaustion, and expected to be prostrated the following day, as before castration, but found myself with vigor of mind and body unimpaired.

Down to seventeen years after castration, there has been no effect on my facial hair. Possibly it has thinned and made more tenuous the hair on trunk and limbs. The consequent deposit of adipose tissue has increased the prominence of my breasts, but before castration these were almost as large as in some women. The operation greatly increased the deleterious effect of fellatio on my health. One indulgence a week was more detrimental than a score a week during my "low-class fairie" period. If I had now been as intemperate as then, I believe I would have become violently insane.

Not until two years after castration was there perceptible a diminution in my craze for fellatio. It was probably the result of the operation, but possibly due to satiety or to age (my thirtieth year). What probably contributed most to my moderation after reaching the age of thirty was the greatly increased deleterious effect of fellatio. I shrank from the penalty of from two to five days of semi-prostration placed by Nature on a half-hour's fellatio. On the other hand, amplexus sine fellatione had no ill effects.

As to the effect of castration on my mental faculties, I am of the opinion—seventeen years after the operation—that there has been no effect either good or bad. I am convinced, however, that the congenital unusually sharp edge of my intellect has been very much dulled permanently by the years of excessive emissions during sleep. But I am *not* convinced that my career as a fairie has contributed. Subsequently to the age of twenty-three I have been a very poor listener, unable to focus my attention, particularly on conversation. Much goes into one ear and out the other notwithstanding my best efforts at attention. It is a species of mental deafness. I hear the words distinctly but cannot grasp their significance. The only other considerable diminution of my youthful keenness of mind is my slowness since passing the age of twenty-five in unravelling a problem, and in arriving at a decision on any matter. For example, as a student, I could see through a mathematical problem almost as "quick as a flash." More and more as I have grown older I am very dense in mathematical reasoning.

To sum up seventeen years after castration—I have always been of the opinion that it was the only thing to have done. But on account of even the slight risk attached to the operation, and particularly the resultant diminution of physical vigor, I would not advise that other inverts be castrated unless they suffer seriously from spermatorrhea.

On my trip to New York in order to be castrated, I had my first opportunity in five months to go on a female-impersonation spree. On the Bowery I met two youthful artillerymen. On our parting they gave me their names and invited me to call at their barracks, which, to obviate notoriety, I will refer to as "Ft. Y." I will likewise hereafter refer to my first military stamping ground as "Ft. X."

Two months after castration I resumed my vocation and residence in New York, and my first care was to dispatch the following:

> O my adored artilleryman,
>
>   I am very sad and lonely. My heart is at the point of bursting through pining for you. I want to visit you at the barracks. I want to see where the dear soldiers sleep and I want to eat in the mess-hall with them. Could you not let me spend a few days with you in the barracks? You can tell the fellows I am your cousin. I wish I could live with warriors all the time. My highest earthly joy is to be in a squad-room and with soldiers. . . What do you see in a girl to love? In a fellow I see strength, boldness, recklessness, pugnacity, a manly walk, and fierceness of expression, which cause me to fall down before him in adoration. . .
>
> Your baby,
Jennie June

After receiving a satisfactory reply, I one afternoon, according to appointment, arrived at the barracks' railroad station. Two soldiers were waiting, but not the two I had met. I inquired if they knew A. B. One replied that he was A. B., and they tried to pass as the two I had met. I declared he was not A. B., but he proved his identity by displaying wearing apparel I had sent him and the letters I had written. I had been corresponding with a total stranger. Nevertheless I accompanied them and they entertained me royally.

They refused to take me to the barracks, as they did not wish to be seen in my company by the other soldiers. They also refused to tell me the names of my two Bowery acquaintances, but inadvertently referred to one by a nickname. I went to the barracks and hunted for its owner until I found him. He received me hospitably. As companionship with soldiers in a squad-room was for me the best of earth's paradises, I had the intention at Ft. Y to conduct myself invariably on the military reservation just like a normal young man, so that I would not be barred from the squad-rooms, as had happened at Ft. X because I had acted the fairie in these rooms.

Nevertheless the fact that I was a fairie spread rapidly, and all eyes were fastened upon me wherever I moved. I learned later that my love letters had been handed around for every one to read. When my call ended, a crowd of fifty soldiers gathered on the porch to see me off. In addition every window was filled with soldiers calling out: "Hello Jennie June!" "Hello sweetheart!" Under such an incentive, I yielded to the impulses of a coquette and gave a female-impersonation, much to the delight of my audience. I was overjoyed at receiving attentions simultaneously from a hundred young Mars. I was never better dressed, blue suit bound with braid—as ornamental as a man not in uniform could possibly wear—and large red bow with ends hanging down below the coat-collar, the bow constituting the badge of fairie-ism. The skin of my face was as soft and smooth as that of a baby, I having only just pulled out every hair by the roots.

Possibly on account of its being just before retreat, only one soldier followed when I took my departure, and one with whom I had never exchanged a word. He scraped acquaintance and demonstrated himself to be an ideal associate for an androgyne. But he was a born and bold robber, ransacked my pockets, and even helped himself to some of my wearing apparel. Nevertheless for the two years following, he was my special partner at Ft. Y, always picking my pockets mercilessly and fearlessly as soon as we met, but otherwise an ideal lord and master. I adored him because he was marvellously handsome, strong, and brave, as well as because he was one of the greatest desperadoes I ever met.

From this date on, in the summer of 1902, until the summer of 1905, which saw the close of my open career as a fairie, I made it a practice to spend an evening (in warm weather generally including the afternoon) one week at Ft. Y, and the alternate week at Ft. X. Having the closest of friendships at both forts, I had thus to divide my time between them. Because of the demands on me in my ordinary scholarly career, I could not give to the "Jennie June" side of existence any more time than that mentioned, although I would have very much liked to be with my idols continuously.

The time that I did spend with the soldiers was almost entirely devoted to innocent frolicking. I was to a large extent the medium through which they got joy out of life. For example, they have given me names of comrades and even of commissioned officers as their own, with the request for a love letter. Until I learned of the deception, the letters went. I was told that my love letters and songs were tacked to the fort bulletin boards in order that every one might have the opportunity to read them. Several times at the beginning of my visits to Ft. Y, I was received in the squad-rooms. Soldiers danced with me there, making believe I was their girl. I was otherwise their plaything, being paraded about on their shoulders or lying in a stretcher, being tossed up in a blanket, etc. I joined with them in base-ball and foot-ball, of course not in regular games, as I was as awkward as the average girl in these sports, being merely the buffoon of the game. Thus taking part in the pastimes of the soldiers was to me one of the highest pleasures of life.

Of course they always regarded me as a girl-boy weakling. Policy required that I always represent myself as a person of no talents except those of the fairie, and as a person occupying a humble station in life. Otherwise some of a vicious turn of mind would have followed me up with the purpose of blackmail, as was done in 1905, when the thirst for money suddenly put an end to my association with soldiers of one fort and almost occasioned my murder. Some quizzed me from time to time in order to ascertain whether I was worth following up, but I saved the situation through subterfuge. While they were ignorant that I belonged habitually to a high social stratum, I lost only trifling sums through robbery and blackmail.

They looked upon me as a rather remarkable individual. One of them told a policeman in my presence that I had been the talk of the fort for months. In a parade in which my soldier friends took part, I as spectator occupied a rather prominent position on the very edge of the line, and from rank after rank as they passed, I distinguished the words: "There's Jennie June." At an inter-fort ball game at which there were 500 spectators, amid the continuous shouting, a score got together on my arrival and several times in unison shouted "Jennie June!" I achieved popularity at both forts, although a small percentage proved irreconcilable.

When soldiers of Forts X and Y met at athletic contests, they interchanged stories about my adventures. At the army manoeuvres in Virginia in 1905, in which soldiers from all the forts in states bordering on the Atlantic took part, my peculiarities and adventures were spread broadcast, as I learned through encountering on the Bowery a soldier from a fort which I had never visited who had just returned from the manoeuvres. Realizing that as "Jennie June" I was very widely known among soldiers, I made it a practice of asking those whom I ran across in New York if they had ever heard of "Jennie June." A considerable proportion, before I revealed my identity, were able to recount adventures in which I had figured.

During this closing period of my open career as a fairie, I was indeed very widely known personally. On the streets and on public conveyances when amid New York's crowds, I was a number of times accosted by young men, some of whom I could not remember, but who had seen me somewhere and knew me as Jennie June. Several times as many people knew me under this name and character as under my real masculine name.

I overran the two military reservations as no other civilian would have been allowed to. Soldiers on or off guard would escort me under or behind the fortifications, beyond the "dead line" for all other civilians. Sometimes at night when I had learned that one of my intimates was on guard on a certain beat, I would seek him. Perhaps I would run up against a stranger on guard, but one who knew me by sight or reputation. A voice out of the darkness: "Halt! Who goes there?" "Jennie June." "Advance to be recognized!" On half such occasions I received the most enthusiastic welcome, and always at least kindness and permission to go on my way.

When I met an acquaintance on guard at night, I would kiss his rifle and bayonet as being the emblems of the highest function of the mere animal man. I would also kiss his gloves and his hat, and shower the rest of his clothing with kisses.

Sometimes I was admitted for an hour or two in the guard-house, where the soldiers waiting for their turn at guard would while away their time in spooning with me, imagining that I was a complete physical puella. I was even introduced near midnight into the prisoners' quarters. To be thus handed over to the youthful military prisoners—in general the wildest and roughest of all humanity—was the attainment of the very height of my ambition as a fairie.

On my departure for home, as high as a dozen have escorted me at night along the deserted country roads and through the woods. Thoroughly fatigued after an hour, and refusing to go on, I would have my wrists twisted, and be slapped and pinched into obedience. But not one of the 500 acquaintances at Ft. Y ever inflicted pain because of ill will, and only six or seven of the 500 at Ft. X. I had remarkable success in winning the favor of men who before learning to know me personally detested me because they thought I was of the type of fairie to be found in the lowest of New York's dens of vice. Personal acquaintance convinced them that I was an individual devoid of all vices except coquetry and dalliance.

In the vicinity of X, I several times came into contact with the police, who came to know me as a fairie. The youthful ones would chat in a friendly manner, but some of the older ones, to whom soldiers who had not learned my inoffensive character had denounced me as an undesirable person to have around, have heartlessly ordered me off their beat, and warned me never to be seen there again under penalty of arrest. I thereafter sought to avoid them, but nothing ever resulted. My conduct in public was of course always above reproach. It was a bitter experience to have the public streets closed to me when I had been entirely inoffensive.

The following are extracts from letters written during this period to a former university associate. He had always been my favorite of all the students, being good-looking, athletic, and of particularly noble disposition. If he had not turned the cold shoulder on my amatory advances, and had been willing to be mated with me permanently—as I fondly imagined before I started on my career as a fairie—monandry would probably have satisfied me for life. In my first two or three years of puberty, monandry had occupied my thoughts rather than polyandry. This friend has continued to be a confidant from my student days down to the present writing, when I have reached my middle forties. In all my fairie life of twenty-five years, outside of several physicians, from whom I sought a cure, and my favorite pastor, I have confided events of that life only to five close friends of my ordinary life, and they all proved helpful and compassionate, and continued to be as good friends as ever.

(1) (Referring to only my second evening spent with men of Ft. Y.) Next they led me to a tree, and said they were going to get a rope and hang me. (Teasing.) I thought they intended great violence, and to save myself, while still held by them, fell to the ground, feigning to have a fit. This ruse frightened them, and they all ran off, fearing they had seriously injured me by their rough treatment. I lay in the woods until they were out of hearing, then arose and walked to the depot. But it was dark and I lost my way, and arrived at the wrong depot. I had my return ticket, which I had kept safe in my sock, but the conductor demanded an extra nickel. I told him I had no money, except a dollar sewed in my clothes.

This I secured and paid him. I told him the soldiers had taken all of my money, and how roughly they had handled me, of course confessing myself to be an invert. It was surprising to hear his words of condolence, coming as they did from an uneducated conductor, the most beautiful words of sympathy I ever heard, just like the words of the Savior to the woman taken in adultery. Among other things he said: "If only every one lived as harmless a life as you, this world would be all right."

(2) I sat down on a stone wall near the reservation to eat my lunch. I was both sick and exhausted, and wept while eating, and regretted I had come when I was feeling ill. But I felt that I couldn't keep away. I longed to be where I am regarded as a girl and a baby, and where I am flirted with and petted. . . I also mourned my fate, reflecting on my errand, and realizing that I was doing what would ostracize me and shock society if they heard of it.

(3) I often ask myself: When will it all end? I answer: When I am thirty years old. (I was then twenty-eight.) Then I shall be no longer youthful, and only a youthful person can be a professional fairie. A fairie over thirty is unthinkable. If I still have strong desire after that age, I shall have to seek some one in private (This came true) instead of flaunting myself as a fairie before the public gaze. For a male of over thirty to act the woman and the baby before a company of men would be unthinkable. But now, at my present age, it seems to me natural and not unbecoming.

(4) I am sometimes conscience-stricken over my actions. When I entered college, I intended my life to be one of self-denial, and I intended in every act to live over again as nearly as possible the life of Christ. But I am now doing almost nothing to spread the kingdom of God in the hearts of men, and to visit and cheer and relieve the afflicted, and I am indulging in so much animal pleasure. . . Nevertheless, though I indulge in promiscuous intercourse, I spend no more moments in the pleasures of Aphrodite than the majority of married people, and I do not make these pleasures the chief aim of life. I spend one evening a week in flirting with what to me is the opposite sex, intensely masculine, fierce, cruel, pugnacious young men, and in dalliance with them. Two hours per week spent in the company of sweethearts, and all the rest of my time spent in seclusion from them. Am I a libertine? Am I indulging excessively in the lower pleasures of life?

I shall now describe a chain of events which led up to my complaining in person to the colonel commanding Ft. X.

Aug. 3, 1903

Adored dark-eyed sergeant,

Please do not be offended because I called you a bad sergeant last night. You were a bad sergeant when you gave me that other sergeant's name as yours, and so made me write that letter to him full of hot protestations of love, all meant for you, but which he was mad to receive. You made trouble for me by it, and the other sergeant threatened to slap me unless I found out your name and told him. So I have told him, but I made him promise not to hit you, only give you a piece of his mind. . . Two months ago you were so friendly to me when you were on guard, and I was more than fascinated with you. The last ten times since that I have been near the fort, I have gone up to the gate to see if you were on guard. Last night I found you there for the first, and I was so glad. But you were not friendly, as you were the first time I saw you, so now I am afraid to write another love-letter to you, for fear you will be mad. . . Why did you let that horrible soldier Murphy hit me and throw stones at me? He ought to be ashamed to hit a girl. . . After I got home, I cried my eyes out because I couldn't come in and talk to you as last time, and because you aimed a gun at me. . . Do please speak to me the next time we meet, because I shall be too much afraid to speak to you. . .

I am, adored sergeant,
Your slave forever,
JENNIE JUNE

About two weeks later I find the same sergeant on guard. Having no fear because of his previous familiarity, I beg to be allowed to spend an hour on the porch of the guard-house, as he had once permitted. But as soon as I arrived there, he declares he gave me permission simply that he might put me under arrest. I beg for mercy: "Do please let the baby go home, and don't arrest her!"

"Hand out a ten dollar bill and you can go home. I won't have you writing such letters to me as you did. Just for one sentence you wrote to

Sergeant V you could be imprisoned: 'I am a woman entombed in the body of a man.' How can you write such things?"

"You cannot complain of the letters I write to you when you have used to me the indecent language you have. I won't pay you anything. You have used language to me ten times as bad as I have ever used to you."

He gradually lowers his demand to two dollars, but I did not have the amount with me. He orders me to lay on the table all the money I have, and it is pocketed by one of the soldiers standing by.

After some time, I felt reassured, and began to act the part of a baby, hoping to put them in a good humor so they would allow me to depart unharmed. Like a four-year old, I beg and pout to enlist so I "can give the soldiers their bread and make their beds." I pout "to be let in to see the sleeping beauties," meaning the soldiers who were in bed in the guard-house. I complain of being sleepy, and sob to be given a bed in the room with the sleeping guard. Artillerymen are repeatedly passing, some of whom tease me rather roughly, pulling my hair, etc. I supplicated: "Do please let me go home and don't hurt me. I am half an invalid and can't stand much."

"You'll be a whole invalid before you get out of here tonight."

"Really I am a semi-invalid. I look well, but eunuchs always look fat and well, even when they are sick."

After I had been detained about an hour, the soldier "Murphy" happens to pass, one of the most burly and roughest in the post. He tries several times to see if he can lift me off my feet by my hair, and though I adore him, I call out just for effect: "You horrible soldier!" He took me seriously. I suddenly felt myself being carried rapidly somewhere. He bore me to the gate of the reservation, and pitched me out on the road. Then he kicked me along for a few feet, crying out for me to get along home, while I was screaming in fright.

About two weeks later, as I was passing the guardhouse, I was placed under arrest by another sergeant-of-the-guard, and conducted before the officer-of-the-day. This was the only time that I was genuinely placed under arrest on a military reservation. The sergeant informed the officer that I was a fairie and that I hung around the reservation and the guard-house. The officer asked me why I frequented the reservation, and I replied: "Because I like the soldiers, because I like to have them for my friends." After an investigation lasting several minutes, when he found out that I had really been guilty of nothing improper, the officer ordered the sergeant to let me go, and in a very mild and gentlemanly way suggested, rather than forbade, that in the future I do not frequent the reservation. He received me indeed in a wonderfully kind manner, for which I shall be eternally grateful to him. Knowing that I was in hostile hands, I appealed to the officer to order the sergeant that no harm should be done me on the reservation.

But the sergeant—one of the few soldiers who detested me— was chagrined that the officer had upset his plan of having me locked up. After the officer had retired, the sergeant therefore started kicking me, and as I ran past the guardhouse, three of the guard, influenced by the example of their sergeant, knocked me down three times. I immediately complained to the colonel. He also received me most kindly, notwithstanding that I explained at the outset that I was an invert, and he reprimanded the sergeant.

A week later I happened to meet "Murphy" on a much frequented street. On my refusal to accompany him to a low bar-room, he dragged me there in spite of continuous protest and struggling. Half a dozen civilians watched the struggle but did not interfere. Inside were several soldiers and civilians, some partially intoxicated and wrangling, and two filles de joie. Before the eyes of all, my captor immediately rifled my pockets, while exclaiming: "I am going to marry you! I am going to marry you! As soon as I get a good drunk on, I am yours!" We were together an hour in the bar-room. Soldiers come and go, some of them flirting with me vigorously before the eyes of all. The next day I wrote my captor:

> O you adored giant artilleryman, Ever since the first time you hit me and drove me out of the gate, how I have adored you! But ever since you carried me out in your arms, I have been wild for you, as I have never been over any other fellow. You have abused me more than any other soldier, but, my cruel master, I adore you the most of any fellow in the world. Of all the men in the world, I would pick you out to be my husband and master. You, fierce artilleryman, are my ideal of manly beauty and charm. You are the ideal I have been looking for all my life. O how I worship you! I pass by the fellows who have always been kind to me, and seek for my husband that one who has been the most cruel. O won't you

take me to be your wife? Last night you promised to marry me before I ever spoke about marrying you. Won't you keep your promise? . . . You are the roughest, fiercest, most daring, most cruel fellow I ever met. That is why I love you so. You are the greatest fighter and slugger I ever met. That is why I am pining to become your slave. . .

A fter my arrest, I did not dare go on the Ft. X reservation for several months. On one of my first subsequent visits—in daylight—I encountered the officer who had mildly prohibited the reservation to me. As soon as he spied me, he walked rapidly in the opposite direction as if fearing I would speak.

In the following year, I was assaulted on the street by three privates because I refused to take a walk with them off into the woods, since one of them had formerly rifled my pockets. I complained by letter to their captain, and he immediately invited me to call. But evidently he afterward spoke of the matter to other officers, and learned my character, for he withdrew his invitation in less than twenty-four hours. Nevertheless I called. I thought it advisable to state in advance something about the peculiar life I led, having no fear of arrest because I never voluntarily rendered myself liable. He frankly confessed that he could not courtmartial my assailants because I was an invert, but courteously ordered all his command to appear before me for identification since I was resolved to try prosecution in a police court just to see whether an invert of unexceptionable conduct on the public street, assaulted by ruffians without any reason, would be there accorded the rights of all other citizens.

On leaving the reservation—much to my surprise—a young woman accosted me and pleaded for my assailants, one of whom was a brother, while she was the wife of a non-commissioned officer. She stated that my assailants solemnly promised never again to molest me, and entreated me not to have them arrested.

Through no resolve of my own, the early spring of 1905 saw the end of my association with men of Ft. X. For several months they were in Maryland, taking part in the army manoeuvres. On their return I did not renew my visits because of taking up my residence in a distant city.

It was with great pain that I paid my farewell visit to Ft. Y. About a dozen soldiers happened to be leaving on the same train, and asked me to join them. When they alighted, I waved from the car window, and they gave in unison and loudly "Three cheers for Jennie June" as the train moved away. Not one, however, knew that I was never to visit them again, as it was not wise for me to make known that I was leaving New York permanently.

At its very zenith—when I held the coveted position of pet of two forts, as I was in large measure—my open career as a fairie now came to an end. After I had removed permanently to a distant city, how I missed the kind greetings which came from nearly every soldier whom I ran across on or near the two reservations, and how I pined for them! I loved them primarily with a Christian, non-sensual, wifely love. With my whole soul I desired to serve them through life as their slave, but my being at the very end of my physical endurance and an unusual economic opportunity in a distant city induced me to say goodby forever. Farewell, a long farewell, to my many soul-mates of both forts!

My songs, in a treble voice, contributed much to my popularity. The soldiers were much diverted, eagerly grasped up the hectograph editions, and treasured and sang them. They likewise preserved love-letters I had written them, and stated their purpose to exhibit both songs and letters to their friends at home when their enlistments expired. The songs formed a large element in my fairie career, as well as describe some of my adventures. Humans, when in love, are inspired to poetize. Some of my own outpourings follow. The dedications are retained as in the original hectograph editions.

(Air original.)

Dedicated to Corporal Frank B.

As I was walking on the beach,
    A corporal did me see;
He said right off, "Dear Baby June,
      Will you my wifie be?"
          I fainted quite,
          From joy, not fright,
    And in his arms did fall;
          I nestled there,
          So free from care,
    And called to him, "My all!"

As we did talk on the sandy walk,
    A private came stalking by;
He said right off, "There's Baby June,
      The girl for whom I'd die!"
          To see him by,
          I had to cry,
    I was so happy then;
          Head on his blouse,
          I breathed my vows
    To both artillerymen.

I took their brawny hands in mine,
    Then kissed till they were sore;
I slapped and slapped each soldier brave,
      These mighty men of war;
          For their love taps,
          And playful slaps,
    I also entered plea:—
          Sweet words they breathed,
          While me they wreathed,
    Down by the murmuring sea.

(Air: "Hello Central")

Dedicated to Sergeant Frank B., handsome, strong, and noble; a brave, brave gunner; the most popular man in his company; the favorite of his captain; first in football; first in baseball; and first in the heart of Jennie June.

Baby is so sad and lonely,
    Pining for her soldier brave;
Night and day, awake or sleeping,
    Crieth for him, e'en doth rave:
O to rest upon his bosom,
    In his blouse her face to hide!
O to feel his strong arms round her!
    Why this bliss denied?

Refrain:
Baby's dying, naught can save her,
    Pining for her brave;
Naught can save but his caresses,
    For which she doth rave:
O come quick, dear soldier hero,
    Clasp her to thy breast;
For she's surely pining, dying,
    In thine arms to rest.

Were she able, surely would she
    Hasten quick to reach thy side;
To thee knit, cemented, mortised,
    Would she e'er henceforth abide:
Clinging, O so fast and closely,
    Would she lose herself in thee;
No more two, but ever, always,
    With thee ONE to be.

(Air: "My Bonnie Lies Over The Ocean.")

The night I first met my fierce Murphy,
    He punched me and kicked me and stoned;
He sent me away all in tatters,
    I screamed and I wept and I moaned.
        But I loved him, I loved him,
I loved him more than I can tell, can tell!
        I loved him, I loved him,
    I loved him more than I can tell!

He was the next time even fiercer,
    He snatched me up, threw me outside;
But while I was held in his clutches,
    My face in his blouse I did hide.
        I loved him, I loved him,
That moment I was in his arms, strong arms!
        I loved him, I loved him,
    That moment I was in his arms!

The third time he said he'd me marry,
    This wonderful, wonderful brave!
I then was so robbed of my reason,
    I nothing did but for him rave.
        I loved him, I loved him,
I nothing did but for him rave—yes, rave!
        I loved him, I loved him,
    I nothing did but for him rave!

I'm dying, I'm dying, I'm dying,
    For love of this wonderful brave;
I'm dying, I'm dying, I'm dying—
    Will he not show mercy and save?
        Dying—dying—
I see yawn for me the dark grave, dread grave!
        Dying—dying—
    Will he not show mercy and save?

(Air: "Sweet Rosy O'Grady")

O Down at Blanco fort, that overlooks the deep blue sea,
    I found a big ferocious brave on guard the other day;
His name is Art McCann, and O, I don't mind telling thee,
    That he's the wildest fiercest Art—that's ever come my way.

Refrain:

>Wild Arthur McCann—
>He's stolen my heart!
>O what a fierce man
>Is this big strong Art!
>I say he looks fierce—
>Fierce, fierce is his face;
>I love wild Arthur McCann—
>In my heart he holds the first place.

He's not afraid of anything, a man more than the rest;
    A man that is a man, enlists, and fights, yea valiantly;
A man in blue!—Red color too is seen upon his breast!
    The strong, the mighty brave, who fights!—who is all boy, all he.

Wild, wild, wild, wild!—I could him kiss forever and a day;
    Strong, strong, strong, strong!—I do adore prostrate upon the ground;
Brave, brave, brave, brave!—I will him praise and every homage pay;
    Fierce, fierce, fierce, fierce!—I would it tell—in all the world around.

(Air: "Old Oaken Bucket.")

Dedicated to J. F. M.

How dear to my heart is the night on that hillside,
    Where we, my dear warrior, did first our love show;
When I on your breast did contentedly nestle,
    While we as two lovers did whisper so low:
How charming you looked in your blue and brass buttons,
    Your belt and your military cap and your part;
Bewitching you were as you put your arms round me,
    And called me your wife and your baby sweetheart.

Refrain:

Your baby girl pines for you, sighs for you, cries for you,
    Moans, shrieks, and dies for you, soldier in blue.

I'll always remember that night on the hillside,
    E'en if, my dear warrior, we ne'er meet again;
E'en though I have many brave beautiful sweethearts,
    You never, ah never, shall drop from my ken:
I'll think of you darling—yes pray for you ever,
    As long as I live on God's beautiful earth;
God gave you to me as a husband so tender,
    You're mine now forever, so much to me worth!

(Air: "The Last Rose of Summer.")

Dedicated to "Curly."

'Tıs a soldier I'm praising,
　　So big and so strong;
The most manly, yet tender,
　　That e'er I did song:
Oh people, you know not
　　The gem that he is!
How can I sing to you
　　What virtues are his!

To fight for his country,
　　He shoulders a gun;
He fears not the bullets,
　　Their whistle's but fun:
Though others might waver
　　In battle's uproar,
My boy shows the hero,
　　A born man of war.

He's the pride of his country,
　　A most mighty brave;
We have fear of no nation,
　　We trust him to save:
With fear he and his fellows
　　The nations inspire;
For they shine out as warriors
　　Of might and of fire.

Though a man of such power,
　　He uses it alone
In causes that are righteous,
　　And ne'er in his own:
He can spare and can punish—
　　A man of such might!—
But is kind-hearted and gentle,
　　Acts ever aright.

　　　　　　　　　　　　　　　　　EARL LIND

He's so kind to the outcast,
    To me whom all curse;
A big heart, sympathetic,
    That never thinks worse
Than to speak kindly words out
    To whome'er he meets,
And assist any sufferer,
    As he stalks through the streets.

And he takes with the maidens?
    They fall at his feet;
They just worship his manhood,
    As master him greet:
O yes he is all glorious,
    In girls' eyes all fair;
His own baby girl boasteth
    His charms, yes, for e'er!

Oh here's to the aughty-aughth company, the finest to my mind,
    The bravest boys in blue and red that I did ever find;
Of all the sweethearts I have met, they are of all most kind,
    In every glory you can name, they have the rest outshined.

Refrain:

They're the finest warriors in the land, in all the world most fine;
The aughty-aughth for my sweetheart, the aughty-aughth for mine.

They are a model band of men, the only such to find,
    Beyond belief fraternal love rules every heart and mind;
They live as brothers in the fort, no brawl, or words malign,
    So brave, polite, magnanimous, surprisingly benign.

Oh noble hearts, oh manly souls, oh men who were born for war,
    Who're ready at your country's call to shed your blood and gore;
Who're ready to protect the weak, and to relieve the oppressed,
    All that's feminine would worship you, fall in your arms to rest.

When the five companies of Ft. X went south, the "aughty-aughth" of Ft. Z acted as guard of Ft. X. On the evening of May 3d I scraped acquaintance. Coming upon a group, I talked and acted more and more like a coquette, greatly to their amusement. I finally started singing my songs, which caused soldiers to gather from every direction, as we were on the reservation. Never before had I received a warmer reception, and I immediately wrote "The Aughty-Aughth for Mine." Contrary to my custom, I was attracted from the city twice a week.

On my sixth visit, there came, suddenly and unexpectedly, a change in their attitude. It came about through a soldier's going over to New York to play the spy. It was the first time in my six years of frequenting the forts. He secured a hold on me through the address which I used in corresponding with soldiers. I had revealed my true name and residence to none of them. Hitherto they had believed I was a nobody, but now discovered that I occupied a fairly high social status. This changed everything. The thirst for money supplanted the desire for a good time with me. Many now felt that they had a grievance because I being well off—as they thought—made them only small presents. They now began to demand that I deliver comparatively large sums, and inflicted suffering when I did not. I gladly gave them all I could—about one-quarter of my income.

After several moderate beatings on the military reservation because I did not hand over the exorbitant amounts demanded, I decided not to enter it again while this company was in charge. They had never dared assault me off the reservation, fearing arrest by the police. On June 3d I was inveigled on in order to be brutally assaulted. The next day I complained in writing to the lieutenant commanding the company. He wrote asking me to call. He immediately laid before me several love letters and songs, of the kind known to my reader, and inquired if I was their author. On my confession, he refused to hear a word about the assault, and sternly warned me never to come on the reservation again. He then ordered my chief assailant to march me off ignominiously, as if I had been under arrest.

Several days later I spent the evening at a resort frequented by soldiers. Many flirted with me, but though repeatedly asked to take a walk, I was afraid to trust myself with any after the serious assault. About 10 P.M., I encountered Sergeant J., who had always been exceedingly kind and twice had let me pass the evening flirting with the soldiers awaiting duty in the guardhouse. I therefore entertained not the least suspicion of treachery and accepted his invitation for a walk. His conduct was of an inflammatory character, and I followed him over a fence into a field, which happened to belong to the federal government, but at the time I gave this fact no thought. The police and the courts had no jurisdiction there. He immediately said: "Do you know you are on the military reservation? What did the commandant tell you would happen if you came on it again? . . . Sergeant W. told me that you told the commandant in his presence that I was the best friend you had in the post. I am now going to show you different." (I had simply referred to him as "a certain sergeant" who had given me the freedom of the guard-house.)

Corporal F., a regular Samson, had been following at a distance. Sergeant J. was just about to be appointed quarter-master sergeant of Ft. Z. Not wishing any charges to imperil his promotion, he had asked his friend F. to inflict the punishment, as the latter's enlistment would expire in three weeks. But the latter had his own grievance also. Two weeks before he and two other soldiers had been torturing me because I had not brought them the sums of money demanded. In order to deliberate without my hearing them as to the next step to take in persecuting me, they had ordered me to run 200 feet to a sharp corner in the path and back again. But I ran a dozen feet around the corner and threw myself in the tall grass. A stone wall too high to climb prevented my getting more than three feet from the path. Because the path was so hedged in, they knew that I could not escape them, and besides we were on the reservation and a sentry was permanently stationed 500 feet around the corner who would surely halt a fugitive. The three immediately sprinted past. In the pitch darkness and with eyes fixed on a point 200 feet ahead where I ought to be, they failed to spy me at their very feet. I immediately arose and sprinted in the opposite direction. In less than a minute I ran into a sentry, but he happened to be a friend and helped me to escape.

On this subsequent evening when I was with Sergeant J., Corporal F. had his first opportunity to avenge my escape. I saw the Samson draw back his fist and covered my face with my hands. But they compelled me to drop them, and I received in the left eye a terrific blow. Five followed on the mouth, nose, and left eye. The right eye seemingly was purposely spared so that I could see to get away. Then my pockets were rifled. I happened to raise a hand to the left eye and felt just below where the eye ought to be a circular protuberance about the size of the eyeball. In my dazed condition I entreated: "Please, please, let this be enough! Don't you see you have already knocked one of my eyes out of its socket?"

They now commanded me to turn my back, apparently being convinced my face could stand no more sledge-hammer blows without a murder resulting. The corporal landed several on the skull, and being evidently a congenital criminal, would have probably kept on until I was dead. The sergeant ordered him to desist, but he would not. The sergeant now had to throw himself on the corporal and hold him from me, while he directed me to hurry off the reservation.*

Reaching a street, I appealed to some civilians, who assisted me to a hospital. For a half hour my face bled profusely and my clothing became soaked with blood. For weeks afterward blood exuded from the nose. My face was all discolored and swollen beyond recognition. As already stated, a former physician, whom I had met intimately several score of times, happened to be a visiting physician at this hospital, and was one of those who attended me as I lay in bed. But my extreme disfigurement prevented recognition, much to my satisfaction, since I had never had occasion to disclose my inversion.

For a month, until my face became presentable, I had to remain away from my ordinary circle. A full description of my injuries was written out by my regular physician to accompany the charges presented several days after the assault to the general commanding the military Department of the East, Governor's Island, New York Harbor. I had to go so high because the temporary commandant at Ft. X was among those accused, that is, for not giving me a hearing when I sought to bring charges against earlier assailants.

I immediately visited the United States district attorney also, thinking my case lay in his province. But he dismissed me after merely remarking that according to law, he could only be on the side of the soldiers and against me. I next went to the police station in whose precinct the fort was situated. I was here received with warm sympathy, notwithstanding that at the outset I declared myself an invert. But I was informed that since all the offences had been committed on the military reservation, the police and civil courts had no jurisdiction. News of the assault had got into the papers, and a police detective had

---

* Some years ago the newspapers told of the killing of an androgyne in Boston by soldier associates.

made an investigation. Both the detective and the police sergeant told me that the commandant of the fort had informed them that I had been assaulted because I had indecently accosted my assailants.

The military secretary at Governor's Island appointed Col. G. to investigate my charges. In the course of the hearing, which lasted about three hours, I appeared to be the one under charges, and was repeatedly insulted by the captain adjutant and the temporary commandant. At its close the latter cried out: "The police are waiting to arrest you as soon as you step off the reservation!" This statement proved to be false. But they succeeded in literally frightening me out of my wits. For the following 24 hours, I had repeated attacks of hysteria, and was actually insane from grief. My mourning lasted for months, because notwithstanding my repeated importuning in person and by letter, they refused to court-martial or punish those who had half-murdered me. The reason was that I had the reputation of being addicted to fellatio.

Approximately two years after castration and one year previous to the close of my open career as a fairie—at which latter date this autobiography has now arrived—I found that my desire for fellatio had perceptibly decreased. In all probability, it was due to that operation, but possibly to satiety or to advancing age, then thirty. Up to about two years after castration I did not pass by a single opportunity except when exhausted. But now I began to reject a large proportion of the opportunities, although I had as strong a craze as ever for association with ultra-virile adolescents who treated me as a member of the gentle sex. I seemed now to be satisfied with simply reclining in their arms, etc. Sometimes during fellatio, I would feel no satisfaction and ask myself why I should stoop to it. If at the beginning of my career as a fairie, my desire had been only of the present strength, I would probably have lived a life of chastity and carried out my plan to be a preacher of the Gospel. The strength of desire was now about that of the average male of thirty—strong, but controllable. For about a year, however, I did not relinquish the open career of a fairie because circumstances had placed me in a remarkably seductive environment. I was also influenced by the desire to make the most of my youth—for at thirty-one I was told that I looked to be twenty-one. A quasi-public fairie career must end before youthfulness passes. I had in advance reconciled myself to semi-chastity, as monandry, after I should pass the age of thirty. As already stated, the saving of my physical and mental vigor was a powerful motive in my weaning. Most of all, my being nearly murdered by soldiers contributed to enabling me to break away from my intimate association with them at the forts. In previous years I had rejected excellent positions because they would take me out of New York and thus put a stop to my visits to the forts. Now in 1905, a few weeks after my disaster at the hands of men of Ft. Z, I was for the first time able to leave New York permanently.

One morning at the close of my association with the men of Ft. Z, I discovered a chancre on the under surface of my tongue. "At last a chancre!" I exclaimed with a slight laugh. It lasted six weeks. Simultaneously at two points the gum of the upper jaw became as hard as bone. Beginning two months later, I would every few minutes during the day for about a month feel a pleasurable thrill in different parts of the body, now in the arm, now in the leg, etc. Four months after the appearance of the primary sore, a second chancre appeared on the under surface of the tongue, only slightly painful, and lasting three weeks. During this time I felt rather ill. It left a small furrow in the tongue, which did not disappear for three years. Simultaneously with the appearance of this second chancre, the skin in the right and left groin, alternately, became very tender, so that in walking the two abutting surfaces would wear each other away. Walking became painful. A disgusting odor was emitted, but daily bathing enabled me to continue my vocation uninterruptedly. Matter exuded from the under surface of the eyelids. I was unable to focus my eyes properly, and sometimes saw double. I suffered from general debility.

I was in despair, regarding myself as at last rotting away with syphilis and perhaps destined to spend decades in a cell in some insane asylum. But I thank a merciful Providence that the state just described lasted little more than two weeks. The abrasion of the skin in the groin alone failed to disappear, but I soon found—on my physician's suggestion—that smearing a little vaseline after each bath prevented all trouble. This precaution has been necessary the bulk of the time subsequently up to this autobiography's going to press (1918).

Before the end of the second year after inoculation, I suffered from two more chancres on the tongue, which did not permanently destroy any tissue. On two other occasions the tongue became considerably swollen without any visible sore, occasioning some difficulty in speaking.

Fourteen months after inoculation four bright copper-colored mole-like spots appeared on the face. The color changed to a dull brown, and they have thus remained a permanent part of me. On several occasions, my body and limbs were dotted with a syphilitic rash, horrifying to see, but disappearing in a week or two and causing no pain or inconvenience.

During the third and fourth year after inoculation, I suffered slightly from "gray patches" on the tongue, swelling of glands in the face and neck, and quite serious syphilitic affections of the lungs and stomach. For several years now I had to use potassium iodide extensively, and with good results. Earlier I had taken only 500 ⅛-grain protiodide pills.

From the fifth to the ninth year after inoculation, there were no symptoms except the abrasion of the groin. For the first nine years, the aggregate amount of suffering caused me by syphilis was approximately equivalent to two five-day attacks of influenza (the "grip"), from which disease I have repeatedly suffered. I am of the opinion that the peril to the human race from syphilis is greatly exaggerated by specialists in venereal diseases. There is little danger from the disease if one totally abstains from alcohol, and possibly tobacco and other narcotics.

But the most serious outbreaks came in the tenth and eleventh years. I awoke one morning to find a small set of muscles paralyzed as a result of a cerebral tumor. The paralysis lasted three months, but these muscles were not entirely restored to normal for two years following. I had simply used potassium iodide in large doses.

Just about twelve months later, I again awoke one morning to find another small set of muscles paralyzed. I immediately received one intravenous injection of salvarsan, and the paralysis practically disappeared a week later. I was disinclined to receive further injections as long as suffering from no serious outbreak. I however kept my system steeped in potassium iodide for several months following.

Each attack of paralysis came at the close of one of the only two periods of my life when I have consumed large quantities of temperance beers (sarsaparilla and root beer), from two to three pints a day. The small amounts of alcohol steadily imbibed apparently brought on the serious outbreaks. Furthermore, both came at the height of the grape season, which fruit, up to the second paralysis, I have always consumed in large quantities. In my case, practically all the serious outbreaks of syphilis came during the grape season.

In the tenth year after inoculation, I was for an entire winter the most crippled person daily mingling with the New York crowds. The rheumatism never troubled me before or since. It immediately succeeded the first paralysis. Rheumatism remedies proved entirely ineffective.

Subsequently to the second paralysis, for the thirty months up to this book's going to press, I have totally abstained from all drinks containing even a trifling percentage of alcohol, as well as from grapes and unfermented grape products. During these months I have experienced no outbreak beyond the abrasion in the groin if not kept lubricated with vaseline. More than ever I am convinced of the truth of the maxim: No alcohol, no syphilis.

As already indicated, three years after castration, my open (i.e., quasi-public) career as a fairie came to an end through my removal to a distant small city where such a career incognito would be impossible. I also now considered myself past the age for such a career, being in my thirty-second year. My suffering from practically total abstinence was now slight compared with earlier periods of isolation, and only such as multitudes of normal individuals endure whom the rules of society compel to celibacy. I no longer lost my self-control, nor was driven into the poor quarters to make a quest under the most unfavorable and hazardous conditions.

In 1907 I had occasion to make a trip in an uninhabited region. My adolescent companions, who had spent a large part of their lives in the wilds of the Rocky Mountains, had prostitutes as the main subject of their conversation. The first hour of our travels, they recognized my inversion, began to refer to me in my hearing as "that—," and otherwise made it so disagreeable that I would have abandoned the travelling camp if it had been possible. . . I tasted such depths of sorrow as not a human being out of a million ever tastes. One evening in particular I wandered off alone in the woods until out of hearing of the camp, though I actually saw that night several bears roaming within a hundred feet. I had a violent desire to die, and did not fear being torn to pieces. Continuously for about an hour, I wailed at the top of my voice over my terrible lot in life, that of a despised, hated, and outlawed degenerate, and over the possibly impending unfathomable disgrace among a party of men from whom I could not at present get away.

Not until after my thirty-third birthday did I attempt coitus cum puella. Up to this time the very thought was too repulsive. This aversion had now in large part passed away, although I had not the slightest inclination. I looked upon it merely as a scientific experiment. Though castration has always been without effect on orgasm when in juxtaposition cum viris, it was now impossible, notwithstanding my companion's manustupration and my own concentration of thoughts on fellatio with my idols. Penetration was of course impossible.

EARL LIND

In 1907 I removed to a city of several hundred thousand inhabitants. As I frequently felt a sense of utter loneliness and melancholia during my two years of practical sexual isolation—for I never indulged in even flirtation with adolescents of my every-day circle—I decided to seek a mate at a military post a few miles from the city. I still longed for a mate to the same degree as the average normal individual.

I had several hundred to choose from, and selected the most attractive, a six-foot, curly-haired, large-boned, blonde athlete of twenty years. I easily scraped acquaintance, and thereafter visited him at the fort three evenings a month, but fellatio occurred at hardly more than one-half of our meetings, chiefly because I did not wish to be intellectually dull the next day or two. The most beautiful sight that I ever saw was this adolescent when accoutered to stand guard. I found that he was by far the most tattooed person that I had ever associated with—for me a great attraction. I also found that he possessed the most charming personality, always treating me most affably notwithstanding that I represented myself—as a safeguard against possible blackmail—as occupying a far lower station in life than the actual. At almost our first meeting I determined to adopt him as my "kiddoson" (combination of son and consort). For the first time, I now, at the age of thirty-three, regarded my particular friend in the son-relation rather than in the husband-relation. But I secretly looked upon him as my husband. Relations were, however, not entirely monandrous, as he brought several of his comrades on our walks.

Not until after sixteen months of occasional association at the fort did I reveal my true name and status, having found that he was entirely trustworthy. He now regularly visited my home, and continued to manifest a most beautiful and accommodating disposition. He was my jewel—the chief thing to me in life. When his second enlistment expired, he was to come and live with me as my "son."

In 1914 business took me back to New York. My "son's" enlistment was soon to expire, and he was to join me there. I had no thought of renewing my visits to Forts X and Y, because practically all the soldiers serve only three years and my friends had doubtless all left. Besides I had become too old (40, though looking to be below 30) for romantic adventures, and my desire for female impersonation had become comparatively weak.

In due time, my "son" came to make his home with me. We shared a pleasant and refined apartment. I had at last obtained an almost life-long desire—to live with an adored young man as his mate. I told him that whenever he was ready, I expected him to bring a wife to our home, and I was to continue to live with them as a parent. I hoped that occasional fellatio would continue unbeknown to the wife. I also told him that his offspring would be to me the same as if they were my own.

But within a few days after we were settled, he, much to my surprise, forbade me to touch him, and insisted that we sleep in separate rooms. My grief was intense. As many as a hundred times a day as I sat in my office or in my home, I had to wipe the tears out of my eyes. Finally he yielded to my tears, and promised that one hour each week I could get close to him, and that all love-making must be confined to that one hour. But I kept an accurate account, and the period averaged only thirty-six minutes a week. I had continually to beg and weep for that morsel of time. I was presenting gift after gift, mostly cash. For every gift, I received a kick—figuratively. He told me that he stayed with me for the six months just for what he could get out of me. He said he could never think of admitting to the bonds of friendship a person abnormal sexually. He would stay in the same room with me an aggregate of only about three hours a week, although I was pining for his mere presence.

He permitted fellatio three times a month, but much preferred the normal with a fille de joie, with whom he spent one night each week, and on whom he spent practically all his money. He stated that he was averse to fellatio because he wished to save all his vita sexualis for the filles.

With the exception of the half-year following my expulsion from the university, this half-year was the most unhappy of my life. The three hours a week that we saw each other were mostly spent in his scolding me and my weeping almost continuously. He would say that he hated the sight of me. Tears were generally running down my cheeks even during fellatio. He had broken my heart by proving to be a traitor to our friendship. But my devotion was not at all lessened. After six months he deserted my home—as stunning a blow as the death of a brother.

But I pursued him and through cash induced him to call on me twice a month for the following two years, when he removed from New York. Several months after he deserted my home, he showed repentance for the way he had treated me while living there. He became as winsome and accommodating as ever, but did not care to live with me again. He said that he could not stand my continual petting. He gave as the reason for his change from winsomeness to an extremely cruel attitude

EARL LIND

the influence of a boon companion in the army, who, after expiration of enlistment, also took up his residence in New York and continued to be a chum and a frequent visitor at our home. This companion was one of the few adolescents who feel an intense and incurable antipathy for an effeminate male, and continually sought to poison my "son's" mind against me, and persuade him to have nothing to do with me.

During the summer of 1916, when my "son" left New York, I became anxious to be possessed of a second. Four evenings were spent hunting in small parks where poor adolescents were accustomed to sit. As I searched I prayed the Heavenly Father to send a suitable adolescent to become my "son." I still shrank from betraying my androgynism to any adolescent of my every-day circle. I desired to reveal it to some brand-new acquaintance among manual laborers, associate with him a few months incognito, and then, if he proved worthy of trust, reveal my identity. Not until the fourth evening did I run across a cleanly good-looking adolescent seated alone—a khaki-clad soldier, my ideal both in respect to type of manhood and in respect to apparel. I immediately entered into conversation. He confided that he was penniless and was spending the evening in the park with the hope that a passive invert would come along and provide him with money. I found him an ideal companion for an androgyne. He had also served an enlistment in the navy, thus uniting the two characters, soldier and blue-jacket, which I have always gone wild over.

After an acquaintance of *only one hour*, because I found him uniquely acceptable, and because he had to leave the following morning for the Mexican border, the agreement was made that he was to be my "adopted son" and come to live with me when his enlistment expired. At the same time I gave him my true name and address.

In the late fall his enlistment expired, and he returned to New York to live with me. The indications that he would prove to be an ideal adolescent to share the apartment of an androgyne more than came true. He was always good-natured and respectful. But he had had no moral training and was an extreme dipsomaniac. He was the illegitimate son of a mistress of a house of ill fame. I did my best to reform him. He would carry away my personal belongings to exchange for whiskey. He refused to work, depending entirely on me for his support.

One evening after we had lived together a month, I returned from work to find my apartment in the condition in which burglars would have left it, locked closets and drawers broken open, and their contents scattered around. All small objects of some value which could readily be pawned were missing. Particularly the carbon duplicate of this autobiography, the ink original having been sent to Berlin three years before and not heard from since on account of the war. I found the following note:

Dear friend Ralph,

My friend over in Jersey City told me to do this what I have done. He may come over to see you tonight or soon, for he says I am doing wrong. He tells me you will get ten years for what you have done. I was drunk when I told him."

I hardly slept that night. It was primarily a wife's sorrow over desertion by an idolized husband, and secondarily the overwhelming fear of blackmail or else of disclosure with consequent loss of economic and social position. Moreover, I momentarily expected that the Jersey City friend—a former soldier—would call, possibly in order to put me under arrest. I kept my apartment in darkness the entire evening as I lay on my bed immersed in the deepest grief. My only utterance was, over and over again: "The Lord hath given, and the Lord hath taken away. Blessed be the name of the Lord."

The following evening I was amazed at learning that the manuscript of this autobiography had been returned by *parcels post*. The package had been inadvertently opened by my landlord, and I therefore decided to confess my androgynism. Moreover, on account of the expected call from criminally-minded blackmailers, it was desirable to appeal to him for protection. His marvellous and hardly expected sympathy greatly relieved my distress. I proposed vacating his house, but he would not hear of it.

The next evening I was amazed at receiving by messenger a letter from my boy to come at once to his succor. I found him in a terrible plight, recovering from a spree. His "pal" had kicked him out of his home as soon as the money was gone received for my belongings. Blackmail and a ransom for my manuscript had been planned, but relinquished when they had skimmed the story of my life. My "son" had only discovered its existence after he broke the lock where it was in storage. I would have immediately taken him back into my home, but my landlord refused to let a thief and a drunkard into the house again. I supported him for another month, but as he rendered me almost continuously unhappy, I then put him on a train bound for his Illinois home.

To those who have not arrived at a correct estimate of androgynism, I state that if he had continued to live with me as my son, his life would have been enriched along all lines, in particular morally and religiously. In practically every act of my life, I have been guided by the highest moral and religious ideals. Outside of sexual delinquencies, my life has been entirely offenceless. An androgyne, even when living out his nature, can attain the same ethical and religious heights as any other individual.

Arrived in my 45th year and at practically the close of my vita sexualis, my advice to the youthful invert just embarking on the journey of life is not to be disheartened over his fate. Nature, as in my own case, will bestow compensating boons for her harshness in this one respect. If instinct is strong, it is advisable to follow it in moderation. But it should hold only a secondary place in life. It should be remembered that Nature exacts a penalty in the shape of impaired vigor of mind and body for practically every sexual indulgence—and perhaps as much of the normally sexed as of her step-children, the congenitally abnormal. Consider whether indulgence is worth the cost in health.

Comparing in 1918 my sexual lot with that of the normal male, I feel that in the matter of the vita sexualis, Nature has been kind to me. She has compensated me for the unusual amount of suffering bound up with the life of the outcast androgyne.

Comparing my sexual lot with that of the normal woman who bears children, I feel of course that she stands on a much higher plane. Her functioning has an exalted end, the perpetuation of the race, and is attended with infinitely more self-sacrifice than is the androgyne's.

Why does Nature make approximately one out of every 300 physical males an androgyne or passive invert? The practice of the ancient Romans, as well as my own experience and that of other androgynes whom I have known, suggests the answer. All patrician fathers of ancient Rome provided androgyne slaves as concubines of their adolescent sons. Marriage with a woman put an absolute end to these relations. In the case of myself and my androgyne acquaintances, practically no man beyond the age of 26 ever sought or permitted relations. The function appears to be to fill in the period between the arrival at puberty and the arrival at the age when it is possible to beget unblemished offspring. With the ultra-virile adolescent, it is often a choice between solitary onanism and androgynous relations.

As this autobiography goes to press in my 45th year, my health is unchanged from what it has been since castration at the age of 28. I am rather feeble, almost a semi-invalid, averaging two days a week when I am in a state of mental and physical collapse. I am, however, an unusually hard worker in my profession during my comparatively well intervals. I have achieved the average business success that comes to university graduates notwithstanding my semi-invalidism and effeminacy. Particularly business has caused me to mingle intimately to a large extent with the very highest class of society, just as my lot has been to mingle intimately and to a large extent with those at the very bottom of the social scale.

As to my personal appearance in my middle forties, my youthfulness is still often commented upon. Recently a new acquaintance, twelve years younger than myself, remarked that he would have taken me, "as for the oldest possible, for twelve years younger than" I really am. I am inclined to think that preservation of a youthful appearance down to middle life is a common characteristic of androgynes. As they are affected more or less with psychical infantilism, this mental trait is likely thus to betray itself somewhat in the physical form. An adult androgyne of my acquaintance has conspicuously the form of skull and face of an infant. Another androgyne acquaintance appears at fifty-five to be under thirty when viewed from a distance of forty feet, but close by his face is seen to be covered with very fine wrinkles such as appear in the face of an ordinary individual only when past the age of eighty.

Having now (1918) arrived near the close of a half-century of life as an androgyne, I find my vita sexualis practically at an end, and feel thereby liberated from an incubus which has hitherto prevented my making the most of my god-given faculties. As I look back on life, I am of the opinion that I have had a "hard row to hoe." In occasional spells of anguish, I have been tempted, like the patriarch Job, to "curse God and die," because He created me a *degenerate*, a person almost universally despised and hated for proclivities and acts for which he is not really responsible. On such occasions, I have also, in the deep gloom which the realization of my perverted nature brings upon me, importuned the Creator to show mercy on me, who have been appointed to such a terrible fate. In my more spiritual moods I shrink from the memory of the experiences through which my abnormality caused me to pass, and am overwhelmed with despair at the thought of the depths of perdition to which cultured humanity consigns the androgyne who yields to his instincts.

I trust that the publication of my life story will contribute to a correct estimate of androgynism on the part of scientists, the molders of public opinion, and the lawmakers, and to a more kindly treatment by society of those born with this curse. It is only expressing half the truth to say that they are more to be pitied than scorned. They are wholly to be pitied.

October, 1918.

Appendix I

IMPRESSIONS OF THE AUTHOR

By a Business Associate

(The editor, although aware of the identity of the writer of this sketch, omits his name upon his request.—A. W. H.)

My acquaintance with the author dates back over eleven years to the day when I commenced work in the same large office where he was employed. We continued to work in the same room and in close association for five years, and have kept up a close friendship for the six subsequent years. On entering my new place of work, he was one of the first persons to attract my attention because of his rather peculiar cast of features. My second distinct memory of him is of entering the office to find him weeping bitterly as he sat at his desk. Since masculine tears are a rather unusual sight, I instituted inquiries and learned that his chief had just called his attention to an error discovered in his work. A third very early memory was of the author's coming up to me, and saying after we had exchanged a few words: "Did you know I am a woman?" After beholding for a moment my mystification, he said: "I was only joking." He went on his way, leaving me trying to unravel the question as to wherein the joke lay.

Other incidents like the two described tended to confirm my original impression that he was a rather eccentric individual, as he was indeed generally regarded by the office staff, who, however, at the same time recognized his good qualities.

About a year elapsed before our acquaintance assumed any degree of intimacy, and it was only after a second year had elapsed that he confided to me his history as outlined in the autobiography. His thus making me his confidant I attribute in large measure to the circumstance that he had learned at a relatively early date that I had read Krafft-Ebing's "Psychopathia Sexualis," and was therefore presumably in a position to give a sympathetic and intelligent hearing. Whether this was the underlying reason or not, it was an important factor in determining my attitude towards him, since the practices consequent on his abnormality inspire me with intense disgust. Only the conviction that he was no more responsible than was Dr. Holmes' Elsie Venner for her obliquity could have induced me to associate on terms of intimacy with one who resorted to such practices. In fact I had been for some years previously acquainted with a man notorious throughout his community for these same practices, but always avoided him whenever possible.

As a matter of fact, it would be difficult for any but the most bigoted, knowing the author of this autobiography, to impute wilful perversion to him. In his general habit of thought, he has always shown an austere morality that caused him at times to be referred to playfully in the office as "Cato the censor." At the same time he displayed in many ways so much guilelessness and lack of worldly wisdom as to make it impossible to believe that this moral austerity could be merely a mask of deep-dyed hypocrisy. It is, in fact, difficult to associate with him without being convinced of his deep religious feeling. Going to church appears to be indeed one of the chief joys of his life. Because it would keep him from the church service, I have even known him to decline an invitation to dinner from an old friend whom he had not seen for several years and to whom he was under great obligations. In fact I have myself come to regard attendance at church services on Sunday as inevitable a feature of my visits to the author's home as it is of my visits to my parents, these being in fact the only occasions on which I attend church.

My characterization of the author's personal appearance would be as mild and ovine (that is, sheeplike). A young lady co-laborer of his in the office said on one occasion when some of us men had been teasing him that he looked "like a frightened bunny." Most persons would probably set him down as somewhat lacking in the more forceful, virile quality. He conveys the impression, as it were, of always being on the point of apologizing for the fact that he exists.

He proved to be an admirable subject for teasing, and some of us at the office got as much fun out of teasing him as we would from teasing and playing tricks on our girl friends, and his reaction to it was essentially feminine—a sort of pleased childlike pride at being the object of attention.

He also at times displayed typically feminine reactions of disgust at repulsive or seemingly repulsive objects. On one occasion, for example, he tore off and threw away the cover of a publication on his desk in the office which had been stained with red ink, because it looked like blood.

In my own judgment, the aspect in which he displays most strongly the feminine attributes is in his capacity for lavishing trust and affection upon unworthy objects. During my acquaintance with him he has at different times had two friends for whom he had especially strong affection, even to the extent of taking them into his own abode; and in one case going so far as to talk of adoption. From his own account of his relations with these young men, the inference which the disinterested listener would draw was that they were persons who were playing a good thing for all it was worth. According to his own statement, they were mulcting him, on one pretext or another, of large sums of money, albeit always on some colorable excuse. He always, however, affirmed their essential goodness of character and refused to believe that they could be otherwise, even when they were acting towards him in the most unfeeling manner. To my mind, in his relations with these acquaintances, he afforded an almost perfect parallel to the woman who, wedded to a drunken brute, nevertheless remains faithful and adoring to the end.

Another somewhat feminine trait is a sensitiveness that is readily moved to tears. I have already referred to the time when he wept over an implied criticism of his work. An equally characteristic episode occurred later, during a visit to his home from his mother. One night he was caught in a heavy rain, and reached home drenched to the skin. The next morning, his face convulsed and tears hardly kept back, he told me of his fear that he was losing his love for his mother because he did not feel like talking to her the night before—as if forsooth a drenching would not have dampened the desire for speech in any man.

One other trait worth mentioning—because it is one that I regard as more or less feminine—is a certain lack of perspective, a tendency to allow minor details to bulk as large in his eye as major. This showed itself in his work, which, though always characterized by thoroughness, was frequently too much so, the really vital things being allowed to become obscured by a mass of detail of minor importance.

May, 1918.

Appendix II

The Case of Oscar Wilde

By the author of this autobiography

Oscar Wilde presents a different phase of homosexuality from the author, that is, active pederasty. Apparently his was the active rôle in pædicatio or inter femora. According to Frank Harris, Wilde's confidant and the author of his best biography, Wilde thus analyzes his penchant: "What is the food of passion but beauty, beauty alone, beauty always, and in beauty of form and vigor of life there is no comparison (with the female sex). If you loved beauty as intensely as I do, you would feel as I feel. It is beauty which gives me joy, makes me drunk as with wine, blind with insatiable desire." "There are people in the world who cannot understand the deep affection that an artist can feel for a friend with a beautiful personality."

Like the author, Wilde was born and reared in the best environment and enjoyed unexcelled educational advantages. But as a boy and youth, he betrayed no feminine mental traits. Unlike the author, he was not feminesque physically. Further, while the author during youth and early "manhood" was notably small, Wilde grew to be one of the largest of men, six feet, two inches in height, and of stout build.

Apparently instinct did not become sufficiently powerful to cry for appeasement until he became a student at Oxford. While one of the leaders in scholarship and already a society favorite, it was nevertheless being whispered that he was a pederast. This was due to his openness, he not seeming to care if every one knew of his penchant, and not realizing that he was guilty of anything scandalous.

Having graduated from Oxford with the highest honors, Wilde took up his residence in London. Unlike the author, he was capable cum femina, but did not marry until twenty-nine. Two sons resulted. Marriage and fatherhood are the two strongest arguments against him in any judgment on his pederasty.

Hardly another human being has at the age of thirty achieved such fame. In the family of the author, then a boy of ten, and living in a different country and 3,000 miles away, the name "Oscar Wilde" was a household term. Even every child of the village was as familiar with that name as with that of the man next door. This fame resulted from his being the idol of England's aristocracy, the greatest social light of the nineteenth century in any land, one of the most brilliant conversationalists that ever breathed, a poet of high rank, and the foremost English playwright of his generation.

But notwithstanding that during the late eighties and early nineties of the nineteenth century, Wilde was the most widely known and the most talked about man in London, he was so disdainful of the opinion of mankind as to visit regularly—not incognito, but under his own illustrious name—the leading maison publique of London which catered exclusively to active pederasts. He here made the acquaintance of adolescents—little better than gutter-snipes—some of whom he subsequently entertained in private rooms of London's foremost hostelry. He also had a habit of leaving his meek, long-suffering wife at home with the children, and taking up his residence in a furnished apartment, where he entertained his adolescent friends. Occasional visits would be paid his wife and children. Some of London's leaders of thought, although at the same time "men-about-town," have been known to exclaim at what they witnessed in the city's drinking palaces: "Is this the great Oscar Wilde who sits, chats, and drinks here with ragamuffins whom he has picked up off the street!"

Blackmail was looked upon as an everyday occurrence. As money both came and went easily, he never gave it a second thought.

Gradually stories of his doings spread throughout all grades of London society. The middle and lower classes soon came to hold his name in abomination, but comparatively few of the "upper crust"—with whom he exclusively associated apart from his nights with adolescent menials—held anything against him because of his almost unrivaled talents and delightful personality.

In 1895, at the age of forty-one, Wilde had reached the zenith of earthly glory. But the puritan element had naturally come to hold him in the greatest detestation. He was thoroughly pagan in thought and in his published works. Particularly was he thoroughly saturated with the writings and ideas of the ancient Greeks, with whom pederasty was common and open. Unlike the author, he had had no religious training, and when adult seems always to have turned the cold shoulder on the Church. Some of his writings were positively blasphemous. He would boast also that for him morality was non-existent—only the beautiful.

While possibly irresponsible to a considerable degree for his pederasty, he was decidedly to be blamed for flaunting it in the face of everybody. On the whole, he was, because of his exalted position and his writings, the most pernicious influence of the 19th century on British morals. The puritan element were quick to take advantage of his arrest under the charge of being a "corrupter of youth," and jumped into the fray. The slums of London were combed in order to find witnesses.

From Harris's *"Oscar Wilde and His Confessions"* I quote Wilde's most striking defensive statement at his trial:

"The 'love' that dare not speak its name in this century is such a great affection of an older for a younger man as there was between David and Jonathan, such as Plato made the very base of his philosophy, and such as you find in the sonnets of Michael Angelo and Shakespeare—a deep spiritual affection that is as pure as it is perfect, and dictates great works of art like those of Shakespeare and Michael Angelo and those two letters of mine (evidence against him), such as they are, and which is in this century misunderstood—so misunderstood that, on account of it, I am placed where I am now (in the prisoner's dock). It is beautiful; it is fine; it is the noblest form of affection. It is intellectual, and it repeatedly exists between an elder and younger man, when the elder man has intellect, and the younger man has all the joy, hope, and glamor of life. That it should be so the world does not understand. It mocks at it and sometimes puts one into the pillory for it."

Subsequently his confidant, Harris, asked in private: "There is another point against you which you have not touched on yet: Gill asked you what you had in common with those serving men and stable boys? You have not explained that."

"Difficult to explain, Frank, isn't it, without the truth?" . . . "How weary I am of the whole thing, of the shame and the struggling and the hatred. To see those people coming into the box one after the other to witness against me makes me sick. . . Oh, it's terrible. I feel inclined to stretch out my hands and cry to them, 'Do what you will with me, in God's name, only do it quickly; cannot you see that I am worn out? If hatred gives you pleasure, indulge it.'"

In other conversations with Harris, Wilde justified his penchant, as narrated in the biography, as follows:

"There is no general rule of health; it is all personal, individual. . . I only demand that freedom which I willingly concede to others. No one condemns another for preferring green to gold. Why should any taste be ostracised? Liking and disliking are not under our control. I want to choose the nourishment which suits *my* body and *my* soul."

"Each man ought to do what he likes, to develop as he will. . . They punished me because I did not share their tastes. What an absurdity it all was! How dared they punish me for what is good in my eyes? . . ."

"What you call vice, Frank, is not vice. . . It has been made a crime in recent times. . . They all damn the sins they have no mind to, and that's their morality. . . Why, even Bentham refused to put what you call a vice in his penal code, and you yourself admitted that it should not be punished as a crime; for it carries no temptation with it. It may be a malady; but, if so, it appears only to attack the highest natures. . . The wit of man can find no argument which justifies its punishment. . . You admit you don't share the prejudice; you don't feel the horror, the instinctive loathing. Why? Because you are educated, Frank, because you know that the passion Socrates felt was not a low passion, because you know that Caesar's weakness, let us say, or the weakness of Michael Angelo, or of Shakespeare, is not despicable. If the desire is not a characteristic of the highest humanity, at least it is consistent with it. . . Suppose I like a food that is poison to other people, and yet quickens me; how dare they punish me for eating of it? . . . It is all ignorant prejudice, Frank; the world is slowly growing more tolerant and one day men will be ashamed of their barbarous treatment of me, as they are now ashamed of the torturing of the Middle Ages."

Harris constitutes himself an apologist for his friend. He outlines a conversation in which he defended Wilde during the time of the latter's imprisonment. After demolishing the argument of a leading English journalist that "any one living a clean life is worth more than a writer of love songs or the maker of clever comedies"—Mr. John Smith worth more than Shakespeare (who was a rake and very likely a psychical hermaphrodite), Harris "pointed out that Wilde's offence was pathological and not criminal and would not be punished in a properly constituted state." Harris is quoted further:

"You admit that we punish crime to prevent it spreading; wipe this sin off the statute book and you would not increase the sinners by one: then why punish them?"

(Another guest of the journalist:) "Oi'd whip such sinners to death, so I would. Hangin's too good for them."

"You only punished lepers in the Middle Ages because you believed that leprosy was catching: this malady is not even catching."

"Faith, Oi'd punish it with extermination." . . .

"You are very bitter: I'm not; you see, I have no sexual jealousy to inflame me."

Oscar Wilde deserved his fall—possibly not because he was a pederast, but because he flaunted his pederasty before the world, and because he was otherwise anti-ethical and anti-religious in the highest degree. After two years in prison, he never again set foot in the British Empire. His wife would never again even see him. He lost all ambition to put to use his extraordinary literary talents. For the rest of his life he made his home for the most part in Paris. Apparently he indulged his penchant more than ever. He remarked once that life would not be worth living if desire should die, as compared with the author's heartfelt wish that it might die in himself. He was constantly pursuing adolescents of the laboring class. He was known to call in to dine with him at a high-class restaurant a dirty, unkempt, but Adonis-faced gutter-snipe. He now acquired syphilis. The chase appeared to be the chief aim of his life, although he now distinguished himself also as an extreme gourmand, tippler, and sybarite in general, not to mention his habitually swindling his old friends out of money.

According to general belief, death came in 1900 at the age of forty-six, and was due to a general breakdown occasioned by gluttony, alcoholism, absinthism, and syphilis. But strong reasons existed why he and his confidants should palm off his death upon the world. In 1918 it is rumored that he is still alive, at the age of sixty-four.

Wilde has given evidence of a slight approach toward feminine mentality. (1) He was unequalled in vanity. (2) During his twenties, he wore his hair in tufts several inches long and partially concealing his ears and coatcollar. (3) He was the most extreme esthete (extravagant feeder on beauty wherever it is to be found, like the author) the world has ever seen. Estheticism and homosexuality are often linked together. (4) At thirty-three he became editor of England's leading woman's magazine. (5) Harris speaks of his "extraordinary femininity and gentle weakness of his nature, and instead of condemning him as I have always condemned that form of sexual indulgence, I felt only pity for him and a desire to protect and help him." Harris further expresses Wilde's reaction to the prison atmosphere as essentially that of a "woman."

Wilde's case suggests an hypothesis: Homosexuality is due to innate abnormal participation in the mentality of the opposite sex. Whether an active pederast or a passive invert results, depends on the degree of feminization. If slight, the former results, who is also capable of heterosexual love and coitus—a psychical hermaphrodite, as was Wilde, who however had a far stronger leaning toward the homosexual than toward the heterosexual. If the degree is high—for example, almost entirely feminine psychically and even inducing feminesque anatomy—a passive invert results, as in the case of the author.

September, 1918.

Appendix III

QUESTIONNAIRE ON HOMOSEXUALITY

(The governments of all cultured lands take from time to time censuses of the blind, the deaf, and other defective classes. None has ever taken a census of homosexualists, although the latter are fully as numerous as the two definite classes previously named, and their effect on the social body is even more marked. The Medico-Legal Journal, on the basis of the following questionnaire, makes the first essay, in the history of culture, in lining up the defective class in question so that science may have a broader knowledge of them than that afforded by the comparatively few detached biographical and analytical notes at present extant. The reader is therefore requested to fill out the following questionnaire—or have the intelligent homosexualist do so—and mail it to the Medico-Legal Journal, New York. If unable to answer all queries, kindly give as much information as possible. Additional schedules will be furnished on request. Unpublished textual descriptions of cases would be welcome, and will be returned on request. The results of this questionnaire will be published, and the addresses of respondents will be filed for due notification.)

(1) Physical sex of homosexualist. . . . . . (2) Age at date. . . . . years (or. . . . . years at death)
(3) No. of brothers. . . . . Sisters. . . . . (4) Approximate age of father at subject's birth. . . . Of mother. . . .
(5) Underline applicable physical type: Brunette. Blonde. Red-haired. Not definitely any of these.
(6) Principal occupation as adult. . . . .
(7) Lineage (i.e., from what foreign countries did forebears emigrate). . . . .
. . . .

(8) Environment in which life principally passed (Indicate by x's):

	Rural or village under 2,500	Municipality 2,500 to 25,000	Municipality 25,000 to 100,000	Municipality 100,000 to 500,000	Municipality over 500,000
Up to 10 years old	.....	.....	.....	.....	.....
11 to 20 years old	.....	.....	.....	.....	.....
21 to 50 years old	.....	.....	.....	.....	.....
After 50 years old	.....	.....	.....	.....	.....

(9) Ever legally married...... Children, how many......

(10) Plays any musical instrument..........................

(11) Underline interest in sport: Practically none. Slight. Extensive.

(12) Underline interest in music: Practically none. Slight. Extensive.

(13) Underline interest in other art (designate): Practically none. Slight. Extensive.

(14) Underline interest in religion: Practically none. Slight. Extensive.

(15) Underline applicable schooling: Less than 8 years. High school. Liberal-arts college. Postgraduate. Professional school.

(16) If liberal arts course, favorite subjects in order of preference.......................

(17) Number—if any—of foreign languages ever spoken with considerable ability..... Number studied for translation......

(18) What—if any—mental diseases suffered ....

(19) A dipsomaniac...... Other drug addiction......

(20) What rather serious (excluding the practically universal) bodily diseases suffered ....
.... Particularly underline applicable:
Venereal warts. Syphilis. Gonorrhea. Locality (initial) of last three..................

(21) If dead, cause of death. . . . .

(22) What—if any—disease has run in the family of either parent . . . .

(23) What other blood relatives have shown sexual abnormality:

      Definite relationship   Nature of abnormality

    . . . .

    . . . .

(24) Are sexual organs normal. . . . . . .   Describe any abnormalities . . . .

    . . . .

(25) Underline applicable fundamental or original instinct:

Fellatio (active buccal). Passive buccal. Masturbation of other. Mutual onanism. Paedicatio (anal), indicating whether subject is active or passive, or both. Cunnilingus (corresponding to active fellatio in the male). Tribadism (corresponding to masturbation of other in the male).

(26) Approximate age when instinct first manifested itself in the feelings . . . . years.   In actions . . . . years.

(27) Secondary or acquired methods of coitus . . . .

    . . . .

(28) Is subject a psychical hermaphrodite (attracted toward both sexes). . . . .

(29) Does coitus stimulate any erogeneous center (i.e., afford a pleasurable titillation of any portion of the body) or is the satisfaction entirely or almost entirely mental. . . . .

(30) State of health day following coitus . . . .

(31) If a male, does coitus induce an emission. . . . . .   If so, is sensation pleasurable or horrifying. . . . .
. . . .

(32) Is there love or adoration for the associate, or is the latter used merely to secure the stimulation of the subject's erogenous center. . . . .

(33) Upper and lower age limits of individuals that attract, with indication of subject's own age at the different periods . . . .

(34) Any quality or apparel (such as plumpness, military uniform) that constitutes a special attraction. . . . .

(35) If a physical male, is he undersized. . . . .   If female, unusually large. . . . .   Muscles vigorous or feeble . . . . .

(36) Is there a striking contrast between the real and apparent age. . . . . .

(37) Any peculiarity about the hair system, particularly the facial . . . .

(38) If a physical male, any tendency to wear the hair several inches long . . . .

(39) Describe any anatomical approach toward the psychical sex (e.g., milk glands in a male) . . . .

(40) Ever desired to wear apparel of psychical sex. . . . .   Ever worn such apparel since childhood . . . .

(41) If a physical male, fondness for loud or fancy apparel . . . . .   If female, for plain apparel . . . .

(42) Ever arrested or imprisoned for following instincts of physical sex. . . . .   If so, aggregate number of months or years imprisoned . . . .

(43) Please note any other significant data as to particular homosexualist on separate sheets.

General Queries:

(44) Approximate number of homosexualists—positively known as such—have you encountered in your life-time: Passive inverts..... Active pederasts..... Male psychical hermaphrodites..... Physically female homosexualists.....

(45) How many additional individuals have been under your suspicion: Passive inverts..... Active pederasts..... Male psychical hermaphrodites..... Physically female homosexualists.....

(46) The author of "Autobiography of an Androgyne" estimates, roughly, *passive inverts* as 1 out of 300 physical males. Please give your estimate: Passive inverts, 1 out of.....males. Active pederasts, 1 out of.....males. Male psychical hermaphrodites, 1 out of.....males. Female psychical hermaphrodites, 1 out of.....females. Other physically female homosexualists, 1 out of.....females. (In query 46, only adults are to be considered.)

NAME AND ADDRESS OF PHYSICIAN SUBMITTING SCHEDULE. THIS INFORMATION WILL BE CONSIDERED CONFIDENTIAL, AND IS ESSENTIAL.

Name............

Street and number...........

Post-office...........

State...........

Date..........

A Note About the Author

Earl Lind (1874–unknown) was a pioneering transgender autobiographer. Born into a Puritan family in Connecticut, Lind—who also used the pseudonyms "Jennie June" and "Ralph Werther"—asked others to call him Jennie as a child, and soon began identifying as an androgyne. As a young adult, Lind moved to New York City and began participating in the homosexual nightlife centered at Paresis Hall. In 1895, Lind cofounded the Cercle Hermaphroditos, perhaps the first advocacy group for transgender rights in American history. At 28, Lind underwent an operation to be castrated, hoping to suppress his masculine features. Although he identified as feminine, the term "transgender" had yet to be coined in Lind's lifetime, leading Lind to self-identify as an "effeminate man," "androgyne," and "invert." His autobiographical works—*Autobiography of an Androgyne* (1918), *The Riddle of the Underworld* (1921) and *The Female-Impersonators* (1922)—are considered pioneering works of LGBTQ literature by scholars around the world.

A Note from the Publisher

Spanning many genres, from non-fiction essays to literature classics to children's books and lyric poetry, Mint Edition books showcase the master works of our time in a modern new package. The text is freshly typeset, is clean and easy to read, and features a new note about the author in each volume. Many books also include exclusive new introductory material. Every book boasts a striking new cover, which makes it as appropriate for collecting as it is for gift giving. Mint Edition books are only printed when a reader orders them, so natural resources are not wasted. We're proud that our books are never manufactured in excess and exist only in the exact quantity they need to be read and enjoyed.

bookfinity™

Discover more of your favorite classics with Bookfinity™.

- Track your reading with custom book lists.
- Get great book recommendations for your personalized Reader Type.
- Add reviews for your favorite books.
- AND MUCH MORE!

Visit **bookfinity.com** and take the fun Reader Type quiz to get started.

Enjoy our classic and modern companion pairings!

Classic & Modern

Printed in the USA
CPSIA information can be obtained
at www.ICGtesting.com
JSHW022334140824
68134JS00019B/1477